Discipleship
or
Pilgrimage?

SUNY series,
The Philosophy of Education
Philip L. Smith, editor

Discipleship or Pilgrimage? The Educator's Quest for Philosophy

Tony W. Johnson

State University of New York Press

Published by
State University of New York Press, Albany

For information, address State University of New York Press,
State University Plaza, Albany, N.Y., 12246

Production by Cynthia Tenace Lassonde
Marketing by Bernadette LaManna

Library of Congress Catalog-in-Publication Data

Johnson, Tony W.
    Discipleship or pilgrimage? : the educator's quest for philosophy
/ Tony W. Johnson.
        p.   cm.—(SUNY series, the philosophy of education)
    Includes bibliographical references and index.
    ISBN 0-7914-2503-7 (alk. paper).—ISBN 0-7914-2504-5 (pbk. :
alk. paper)
        1. Education—United States—Philosophy—History—20th century.
    2. Dewey, John, 1859–1952.   I. Title.   II. Series: SUNY series in
philosophy of education.
    LB14.7.J65   1995
    370′.1′09730904—dc20
                                                            94-28018
                                                              CIP

*This book is dedicated to my many teachers—
among them Professors Gurney Chambers, Kenneth Cooper,
Robert Polk Thomson, and Jack Conrad Willers—who are significantly
responsible for whatever wisdom that appears in this volume.
It is also dedicated to my loving wife, Fran Johnson,
for teaching me the value of collaboration.*

Contents

Notes from the Series Editor

The series in which this book appears was initially envisioned as "New Directions in Philosophy of Education." In a manner of speaking, Tony Johnson's work is more about the past. It provides an eloquent portrayal of the issues, ideas, and personalities that have dominated philosophy of education over the last seventy years. Yet, it would be a mistake not to see this work as focused primarily on the future. It is about what philosophy of education might be, what it has always tried to be, sometimes with inspiring results.

Johnson describes his initial substantive encounter with philosophy of education that occurred during his first year as a graduate student. Jack Willers was the teacher and G. Max Wingo wrote the text. Together they provided Johnson with more than a solid base of information and a conceptual understanding of the literature of this field. "Professor Willer's love of wisdom was contagious, and he personified the detailed analysis of ideas and persistent sense of wonder that characterizes genuine philosophy." Willers used Wingo's text as a springboard for stimulating students to think with greater sophistication about the things that were important to them.

The significance and contribution of Wingo's text, apart from Willer's use of it, was apparent to Johnson only after he became a teacher of philosophy of education. The text gives to serious and not-so-serious students alike something to help them fit together the things they read, the things they hear in lecture, and the practices they observe in school. As Johnson notes, "the intent of the text is not to provide students with the answers but to enable them to understand the basic questions of the field and to stimulate investigation into issues or problems that may be introduced or treated superficially in the text." Students almost always come away from this book believing it has given them a deeper conceptual grasp of contemporary educational practice, especially in the United States.

Wingo does not make simple-minded associations between the abstractions of philosophy and the actions of educators. But neither does he suggest that there are no associations to be made, or that it is a matter of the individual's subjective imagination to construct them. Either one of these attitudes would be an insult to philosophy, which explains why philosophers of education up to the present day when pressed for the relevance of their work so frequently fall victim to simple-mindedness. Wingo's approach is to "construct a comprehensive view of educational activity in *its social context*" and to do so by means of philosophical dialogue among and between the diverse traditions of our culture.

The viture of Willers as a teacher and Wingo as a text is that, in addition to knowing what needs to be done, each is wise in knowing how to proceed. Johnson's virtue is the same, except that instead of talking directly to all educators about their philosophical roots he is talking primarily to those of us who have become, sometimes by default, the stewards of the great conversation about the relationship between education and culture. Johnson makes it clear to us, as Willers and Wingo did to their audience, that for all of its foreboding prospects, responsibility for the future is in our own hands.

Philip L. Smith

Foreword

Wrapped in equable prose though it be, Tony Johnson's book contains an explosive thesis: that philosophers of education make assumptions about knowing, learning, and the value of professionalism that are self-defeating and educationally destructive. In delineating these ironies, Johnson deepens the critique of the professionalized, departmentalized university.

Consider the role that John Dewey's thought has played in the development of professionalized philosophy of education. He is one of the great philosophers of this century; the role of education is absolutely central and organic in his thinking—the heart of it, really; most educators claim to respect him highly; he is supposed to have had a great influence on education.

Yet, even while Dewey was writing his most important books in the teens, twenties, and thirties, influential educators were abandoning—whether intentionally or not—his most fundamental root ideas. Echoing and augmenting Plato, Dewey believed that philosophy is just systematic thinking about the process of education itself. How do we learn to live in the world in the most fulfilling and humane way, and how does this involve communication between young and old? A daunting question, as Plato's teacher Socrates had seen: we can only be *lovers* of wisdom (as the word *philosophy*—philo-sophia—itself suggests), not professional specialists boasting the authority of final answers—only dedicated amateurs (ama-teurs).

The decay of traditional authorities in our century leaves a kind of vacuum, and most of us reveal a deep need (perhaps a panic need) to be authorized within some social structure. Typically today it is a professional structure with the appearance, if not the substance, of "scientific process and organization." "Philosophers of education" (professionals must have some title!) are no exception.

And of course, there was an overarching authority-structure: "pure philosophy" as it was being organized professionally at this time—the American Philosophical Association. An what was happening in that august group? They were busy elevating their subject into "pure theory"—theory uncontaminated by "application or practice," which included social action *and* teaching. The first president of the APA, Professor J. E. Creighton, said in his inaugural address: "I would like to express my opinion that it would be a mistake to make the discussion of methods of teaching philosophy a coordinate purpose, or even to introduce papers on this subject into the programme of the meetings."

But for Dewey (and a number of other important philosophers) philosophical theorizing that amounts to anything is always theorizing about practices—explicit or implicit—particularly the practice of teaching and learning, education! Johnson lays out methodically how philosophers of education were drawn—so ironically—into this trap. To be authorized and gain social standing they fitted themselves into professional structures. But these structures were drifting ever farther from the educators' own subject matter: the attempt to think comprehensively about the always "amateurish" struggle for wisdom. Johnson writes,

> In attempting to become as academic as possible, educational philosophers alienated their natural colleagues and never gained full acceptance by academic or "real" philosophers. In hitching their wagon to the . . . professionalized vision of philosophy, educational philosophers not only denied their reason to be, but ensured for themselves a lonely, inconsequential professional or academic life.

This is no time to itemize what "pure" philosophy has become today in professionalized departments: the tedious reification of abstractions such as "propositions," and their manipulation in formal or quasi-formal systems; constricted theories of truth and straitened philosophical psychologies, etc. Though they are American philosophers, few of those in "the best" departments—that is, "analytic" ones—take classical American philosophers, pragmatists or idealists, seriously. Though they are philosophers who are paid to be educators, few give any serious attention to philosophy of education—and of course will not dirty their hands with "philosophers of education." I would guess that forty-nine out of fifty PhDs freshly minted from "the best" graduate departments of philosophy today cannot talk intelligently for three minutes on John Dewey (or certain other seminal figures in the history of philosophy). That many philosophers in departments of education still, apparently, try to ape this state of affairs is pathetic and destructive.

What of the "neo-pragmatism" of Richard Rorty, and how it has caught on in "post-modern" and "deconstructionist" circles in the university? I agree in general with Johnson's treatment of this movement. To think that it furthers Dewey's project of reconstruction in philosophy and education is absurd. Rorty says some interesting and timely things. But he guts Dewey of his real—metaphysical and existential—punch, and refuses to face the deepest issues left to us by the pragmatists—truth, learning, self, subconscious experiencing, technological society, the depths of consumerism and alienation—all that we must face if we would be serious educators. Rorty is preeminently a disillusioned analytic—and verbalistic—philosopher.

Johnson's last chapter is fitting: "Educational Philosophy: Discipleship or Pilgrimage." Even a great philosopher such as Dewey cannot be slavishly copied. Never has personally invested, daring philosophical grappling with educational issues been more needed. To do this philosophers of education must indeed "detach themselves from professional philosophy," as Johnson says. My only qualification: professional philosophy *as currently constituted*. I don't want to believe that professional philosophy cannot ever change. If we do not believe that it can, it certainly cannot. It is only reasonable to hope that it can, and to work toward that end.

I commend this book to your close attention.

Bruce Wilshire
Rutgers University

1

Introduction and Overview

Philosophers have always been concerned with educational matters, but as an academic specialty, the study of educational philosophy is a twentieth century phenomenon. Though its roots in the United States can be traced to the nineteenth century, the emergence of educational philosophy as a field of study parallels the development of schools and colleges of education in the modern American university. The intent of this study is to both examine and interpret the roots of the field and to chronicle its development during this century.

James Kaminsky suggests that educational philosophy as we know it began with the establishment of the John Dewey Society at the Hotel Traymore in Atlantic City, on Sunday, February 24, 1935. To others it began in 1941 with the founding of the North American Philosophy of Education Society. According to this view, the discipline of educational philosophy "did not begin until the genius and literary style of philosophy by a 'learned guild' (was established) for the purpose of supplying a specific research program consistent with the intellectual ambitions of said 'learned guild'."[1] Such a narrow view of educational philosophy and its origins not only confines the field to a limited, professional role, but, ironically, denies the creative and integrative role that John Dewey envisioned for this emerging field of study. In embracing this narrow, more professional role—in preferring what Harold Rugg labels "the conforming way" to the "creative path"—the field chose academic respectability over social relevancy.

In *The Teacher of Teachers*, Harold Rugg suggests that in choosing the "conforming way," those responsible for preparing prospective teachers, including educational philosophers, became apologists for the status quo rather than leaders of a creative citizenry building a genuine democratic society. As Rugg argued more than four decades ago, educational philosophers and others responsible for fashioning university programs for the training of teachers became "the spokesman for the Practical Men and got their education as worshipful students of the Victorian exponents of the liberal arts."[2] As educational philosophy emerged as one of the last social sciences evolving out of the old moral philosophy course, this new discipline retained much of the conservatism associated with this capstone course of the "old time college." With the emergence of the university as the dominant form of higher education in the United States, this Victorian liberal arts tradition—what Laurence Veysey labels as liberal culture—and advocates of a seventeenth view of science joined together in support of the "conforming way."

As a result, educational philosophers and other educators have yet to fulfill their potential as change agents, responsible for guiding the "culture-molding process."[3] Aware that the concepts of a more creative way had been outlined by John Dewey and other late nineteenth and early twentieth century thinkers, Rugg remained optimistic. Recognizing that his predecessors chose not to take advantage of the opportunity to follow the "creative path," Rugg believed that the time had come for educational philosophers and others responsible for the training of teachers to assume their rightful place as the true creative leaders of a genuine or strong democracy. It is difficult to share Rugg's optimism in light of educational philosophers' continued reluctance to marshal their considerable knowledge and skill to the task of fashioning prospective teachers as society's change agents committed to and capable of building a strong democracy. It may be too late, but, since the future is not preordained, I choose to remain optimistic that there is still time to revive a largely moribund field. In concert with Rugg's vision of what educational philosophers could and should be, this examination and interpretation of the study of educational philosophy will hopefully contribute to the renewal of the field.

Speaking in the midst of the Cold War, Rugg suggests that for democracy to survive and prosper, "the schools and colleges must become public forums on public issues."[4] To conduct these forums, the talents of those imbued with the spirit of the creative path are required. Teacher trainers committed to the creative path must use their imagination, "based on their encyclopedic knowledge of the new university disciplines,"[5] to assist the public in resolving common problems. Only such trainers of teachers have or can attain the integrative knowledge and experience to achieve these goals. Only liberally educated but vocationally oriented educational philosophers are capable of performing this very public educational role.

Rugg's vision of the role that trainers of teachers should play in a democracy provides educational philosophy with a model worthy of emulation. Just as Rugg thought of his work as a mirror to reflect what the teacher of teachers could become,[6] it is my hope that this work on the study of educational philosophy encourages current and future educational philosophers to reflect on what the field can and should be.

In constructing this image of the field of educational philosophy, the nineteenth century origins of this twentieth century academic discipline are explored. As part of this exploration, the role that philosophy played both in the "old time college" and the modern American university is explained. Not surprisingly, educational philosophy has been largely and understandably derivative of philosophy in general. To illustrate this dependency, a historical explanation of the "implicative" and "applicative" views of educational philosophy is presented. To the extent that the identity of educational philosophy remains associated with the parent discipline, the professionalization of one meant the professionalization of the other. With the professionalization of philosophy and educational philosophy, enlightenment thought reached its zenith. In more recent times, the triumph of enlightenment thought has been condemned by the postmodernists. Both this drive toward professionalization and the postmodernist critiques of it are significant themes developed in this work.

Following this historical discussion of the past and present status of educational philosophy, suggestions for reconstructing the field into an autonomous, expansive discipline are offered. While no blueprint for such a transformation is possible, John Dewey's ideas are mined for clues for reconstructing the implicative and applicative versions of educational philosophy into philosophy *as* education. After discussing the Philosophy for Children approach as a possible exemplar of what philosophy *as* education could be, the work continues by suggesting that as long as educational philosophy remains parasitic upon the parental discipline, it will be forever susceptible to the perils of discipleship, i.e. mimicking the insights of the great thinker or uncritically accepting the truths of a particular philosophical system or approach. When this occurs the philosophic spirit is denied and critical and creative thinking ceases. As an alternative to discipleship, the concept of philosopher as pilgrim is introduced. Like a pilgrim, the autonomous philosopher as educator pursues a never-ending quest for meaning. Each of these themes is developed more fully in one or more of the following seven chapters. Offered below is a brief overview of each of these chapters.

In chapter 2, "Nineteenth Century Origins of Educational Philosophy," a brief discussion of the nineteenth century "educational philosophies" that provided the foundation for this emerging field is offered. J. J. Chambliss suggests that the writings of the inductive empiricists, rationalists, and naturalistic empiricists provide us with a small body of literature that indicates that by 1913 the discipline of educational philosophy was firmly established in the minds of serious students of education.[7] The purpose in examining these nineteenth century foundations for this twentieth century academic discipline is to increase our understanding of not only what educational philosophy has been or currently is, but what it might become.

One can find in each of these educational philosophies the necessary elements for a new synthesis in educational thought, but as Cornel West explains, the roots for such a synthesis can be found in the thought of Ralph Waldo Emerson. If the philosophical pieces were in place to establish educational thought into what several contemporary authors refer to as philosophy *as* education, the question becomes why did the emerging field of educational philosophy deny this Deweyian and Emersonian vision for the more conservative "conforming way." In search of an answer to this and related questions, the impact of the old-time college's capstone course in moral philosophy is discussed.

Defined "as the science that teaches men their duty and their reasons for it,"[8] the moral philosophy course aimed at assisting young men in distinguishing right from wrong and at illustrating, through reason and revelation, the inherent unity of all knowledge. As the new social sciences, including educational philosophy, evolved out of this course, the question became whether the ethical and unifying elements of this once powerful course would or could be carried on by its successors.

The capstone course in moral philosophy disintegrated as the modern university emerged as the dominant form of higher education in America. In discussing the origins of educational philosophy, the linkages to social and moral philosophy must be considered, but the emergence of the social sciences and their relationships to the social reform movements of the late nineteenth century cannot be ignored. During the latter half of the nineteenth century social science and social reform movements joined forces in an attempt to solve the problems brought on by the forces of industrialization and urbanization. While the relationship among and between these emerging scientific, social disciplines and extant social reform movements is both subtle and complex, it contributed to educational philosophy, along with various social sciences, finding its "way into U. S. universities."[9]

While the bureaucratic structure of the modern university was well established by the end of the nineteenth century, schools or colleges of education housing departments of social foundations, including educational philosophy, did not emerge until the opening decades of the twentieth century. As this occurred and to the extent that educational philosophy retained its ties to the old moral philosophy course, it is not surprising that educational philosophers and others responsible for devising programs for the training of teachers chose what Harold Rugg calls the "conforming way."

From the collective perspective of these prominent educators, the purpose of education was to pass on to each new generation the best the western world had to offer. Of particular significance for the field of educational philosophy is the role that Nicholas Murray Butler played in teaching educational philosophy at Teachers College, Columbia in the 1890s. Butler's graduate level Principles of Education course, in conceiving of education as "the adjustment of the individual to the world,"[10] was representative of the field of educational philosophy from its development in the 1890s up to World War I. The philosophers and educators involved in creating new fields and new professional programs did not share those advocating the "creative path" view of education as a process of recreating and rebuilding the world into a better place for all humankind. A generation later, as discussed in chapter 3, the ideas associated with the "creative path" would be briefly considered, but eventually educational philosophy joined its parent and other social sciences in becoming just another specialized and professionalized academic discipline.

Chapter 3 focuses on educational philosophy during the first three-quarters of the twentieth century. In this century educational philosophy emerged as a distinct discipline, developing in tandem with the schools and colleges of education in the modern American university. It is ironic that, during its infancy, educational philosophy ignored the warnings of Dewey and mimicked its parent at a time when philosophy itself was experiencing an identity crisis. Barrett and others characterize philosophy in the early decades of the twentieth century as rebelling against the classical rationalism of the previous century.[11] With rationalism on the wane and pragmatism unable to replace it as the dominant philosophical tradition, the academic study of philosophy focused temporarily on a comparative study of the "isms." Following the lead of the parent discipline, many educational philosophers taught courses and published texts introducing students to various and often competing philosophical systems or "isms." John S. Brubacher, of Yale University, championed this comparative approach as the corrective for the professional astigmatism resulting from a too narrow view of educational philosophy.[12]

The "isms" and related approaches dominated the field of educational philosophy until midcentury and are still common in many less research-oriented institutions. Giarelli and Chambliss characterize this approach as the "implicative" or "philosophic positions" view of educational philosophy. From this perspective, educational philosophy serves two masters; the community of academic philosophers on the one hand and the community of practicing educators on the other. In short, this is philosophy *of* education.[13]

By midcentury, there was general agreement that there was not enough philosophy in the philosophy of education. With philosophy in general embracing logical and linguistic analysis as *the* philosophical method, the call by Harry Broudy and others prominent in the field for more philosophy in the philosophy of education contributed to this still embryonic discipline "shifting its attention to the logical and linguistic analysis of educational concepts and problems..."[14] In embracing what Giarelli refers to as the "applicative" approach to educational philosophy, the field did not free itself from its dependency upon philosophy in general. This philosophy *and* education approach, when done well, has much to offer the field of educational philosophy. When done poorly, scholasticism, not increased understanding, is the result.

As the strengths and weaknesses of these two approaches are explored, G. Max Wingo's *Philosophies of Education: An Introduction*, and Jonas Soltis's *An Introduction to the Analysis of Educational Concepts* are discussed. To explain my preference for the Wingo approach to the study of educational philosophy, Kieran Egan's suggestion that learning "is the dialectical process of forming opposites and mediating between them" is introduced. "For example, in learning the temperature continuum, children tend to learn binary opposite concepts of 'hot' and 'cold.' Next they mediate between these and learn the concept 'warm.'"[15] Students using the Wingo text encounter increasingly complex variations of the conservative-liberal binary opposite. As students enter the dialogue between those championing the principles of educational essentialism and its challengers, they begin to relate the conflicts discussed in the text to their personal and professional problems and begin to develop their own unique perspectives on the key questions.

While recognizing that the analysis of educational concepts is an important and worthy objective, Soltis's claim that philosophical analysis needs to precede the study of "isms" is challenged. It is suggested that such a claim is akin to the notion refuted by Egan that children learn best by proceeding from the concrete to the abstract, from the simple to the complex, and from the known to the unknown. This chapter concludes by suggesting that for educational philosophy to achieve its full potential, it must abandon the notion that it is a hierarchical and specialized field.

As explained in chapter 4, educational philosophers continue to view their field as a rather elite and somewhat distinct discipline. Their embrace of professionalism can be traced, suggests Bruce Wilshire, William Barrett, and others, to the organization of the American university around a seventeenth-century conception of knowledge. If philosophy, the field that traditionally knew no boundaries, could be professionalized, then it could happen to any field. The modern American university, in organizing itself in accordance with a Cartesian view of knowledge, committed itself to the specialization and professionalization of academic disciplines as the divisions of knowledge follow "inexorably and rapidly" from "the broad outlines of Cartesian psycho/physical assumptions."[16]

This move toward professionalism swept the United States in the late nineteenth century. Americans, more so than any other modern society, embraced professionalism for it allowed them to distinguish between individuals and groups without relying on traditions or barriers common in Europe and other more traditional societies. As the emerging middle class in America embraced professionalism as the replacement for the 'jack of all trades' amateur, they looked to the university to train and credential these new, scientific experts. Lacking or rejecting traditional forms of authority, Americans readily embraced science as their new metaphysics. Since professionals routinely justified their actions by appealing to scientific fact, the function of the university became one of discovering or producing "universal scientific standards credible to the public."[17]

With the demise of the old moral philosophy course, most academic philosophers, in an effort to survive in the scientifically oriented university, chose to emulate the sciences by professionalizing the disciple. As illustrated by the development of the American Philosophical Association, this drive toward professionalization triumphed during the first three-quarters of the twentieth century. What began in 1902 as an intimate association between fifteen colleagues evolved into an 8,000 member organization where hundreds of papers are presented at the national meeting each year. What J. E. Creighton and others envisioned as a collegial, albeit tough-minded discussion among a relatively small group of professional philosophers has evolved into a cold, lifeless process more concerned with advancing the prestige and credentials of the participants than in contributing to the educational goal of fostering greater understanding of truth or meaning.

During the 1930s and 1940s, educational philosophers ignored the warnings of John Dewey and mimicked the parent discipline by establishing learned guilds "for the purpose of supplying a specific research program consistent with the intellectual ambitions of said 'learned guild'."[18] The first of these organizations, The John Dewey Society, has survived for almost six decades by vacillating between the social activism advocated by many of its original founders and by mimicking other professional associations promoting academic disciplines. If, as suggested here, The John Dewey Society reluctantly succumbed to the pressures of professionalization, the Philosophy of Education Society (PES) willingly embraced professionalization as the vehicle that could bring this emerging field academic respectability. This desire for academic credibility became an obsession to some, resulting in rather peculiar sessions at the annual PES meetings. As many members sought to outdo the "pure" philosophers, Ernest Bayles recalls "few programs dealing directly and forthrightly with problems of education."[19] Throughout its history, the Philosophy of Education Society has been an exclusive and somewhat arrogant group. In its attempt to raise educational philosophy to equal status with real or "pure" philosophy, PES has become an almost textbook example of a national association advocating the professionalization of a field.

There is some evidence that these philosophical/professional associations are interested in reestablishing the connection between philosophy and pedagogy. While this is a welcomed step in the right direction, it is not the panacea for the problems associated with professionalism. What is needed, suggests Ernest Boyer, is a reconsideration of the priorities of the professoriate. Specifically, Boyer recommends that universities recognize the scholarship of integration, application, and teaching as equal to that of discovery or traditional research.[20] While philosophy proper and educational philosophy are well suited for the scholarship of integration and application respectively, the scholarship of teaching is natural to both fields. Teaching that is done well, that is, teaching that involves transforming and extending as well as transmitting knowledge, is scholarship of the highest order.

Structural changes within the university are required if the scholarship of integration, application, and teaching are to be valued, but educational philosophers must reorient themselves more toward the schools if they are to satisfy their reason to be. Their "reason to be" is to contribute to the development of teaching as an honorable profession. The ultimate irony is that for educational philosophers to fulfill their field's potential, they must abandon efforts to develop their field into a distinctive and professionalized academic discipline.

If twentieth-century philosophy is a revolt against rationalism, chapter 5 is concerned with the extension of that revolt to rationality itself. In a sense, these "Postmodernist Critiques of Philosophy and Educational Philosophy" represent a revolt against the excesses and arrogance often associated with twentieth-century manifestations of Enlightenment thought. At its most basic, it is a "distrust of Metanarratives"[21] that defines the postmodernists attitude. The question of central concern here is: after effectively deconstructing the modern world and its institutions, do postmodernist have the energy and vision to reconstruct that which they demean and despise? It has been suggested that postmodernists are travelling along a path blazed by John Dewey, but it remains to be seen whether these postmodernist critiques lead to a revival of the critical pragmatism of Dewey or serve as an apology for contemporary bourgeois liberalism. These questions are fleshed out in this and the following chapter.

To illuminate the significance that postmodernism has for philosophy and educational philosophy, the thought of Richard Rorty is discussed. With the publication of his seminal work, *Philosophy and the Mirror of Nature*, postmodernist themes entered the philosophical mainstream. Rorty is critical of modern philosophy's infatuation with science. This infatuation has resulted in epistemology assuming an increasingly significant role in the field of philosophy. In short, this infatuation with science has resulted in "the desire for a theory of knowledge (which) is a desire for constraint—a desire to find foundations to which one might cling, frameworks beyond which could not stray, objects which impose themselves, representations which cannot be gainsaid."[22] Rorty's critique of this desire for constraint is reminiscent of Dewey's *The Quest for Certainty*, but, unlike Rorty, Dewey offers a reconstructive vision to go along with his criticism of the world as it is.

Rather than thinking of philosophy as foundational, Rorty prefers to think of it as a poetic, edifying enterprise "designed to make the reader question his own motives for philosophizing rather than to supply him a new philosophical program."[23] Unlike more systematic philosophers who construct arguments designed to prove or persuade, edifying philosophers employ the tools of artists, offering satire, parodies, and aphorisms to help others to learn from their own as well as from the mistakes of others. At their best, Rorty's edifying philosophers approximate the Socratic philosopher helping others to improve by learning from past mistakes. At their worse, edifying philosophers, in failing to develop a vision of what could and should be, become apologists for the status quo.

Rorty suggests that "staying on the surface, philosophically speaking"[24] promotes political freedom. Rorty speaks with pride of our (presumably western democratic) culture's reliance on the mechanics of procedural justice in handling sticky moral and legal problems. Since no one has or can have a God's eye view of such matters, the best we can do is to muddle-through, relying upon procedures that have been developed and revised over time. Rorty is on target in cautioning against philosophers' tendency to seek the God's eye view, but provides the philosopher with only two options; either become a cynic convinced that progress is impossible or become a playful amateur, content with illustrating the absurdities of our modern existence. Rorty favors the latter role, but in either case the edifying philosopher is impotent, incapable of inspiring humankind to create a better future.

In chapter 5, the ideas of Richard Rorty and other postmodernists are compared to those of John Dewey. In chapter 6, it becomes clear that Richard Rorty is no John Dewey. To Dewey, philosophy could and should do more than just "keep the conversation going." Still, Dewey was not pleased with the direction modern philosophy, including educational philosophy, had taken. Dewey believed professional philosophers "spent too much time trying to perfect their techniques or arguing about philosophical systems of the past."[25]

In the decades following World War II, the field of educational philosophy grew dissatisfied with the "isms" approach and began searching for *the* philosophy of education. Rather than embracing Dewey's view of philosophy as "the general theory of education," the field as a whole mimicked the parent discipline and adopted the analytic approach to educational philosophy. Dewey's notion that serious young men would use philosophy more in the study of "indirect sociology" than professional philosophers do suggests something was seriously wrong with his chosen field.

Born in 1859 in puritan New England just as Darwin's *Origins of the Species* was being published, Dewey died in 1952 as the nuclear age and the Cold War emerged full blown on the global scene. As suggested by his autobiographical "From Absolutism to Experimentalism," Dewey gradually recognized that his commitment to democratic principles could be sustained by grounding them in experience. Attaining his undergraduate degree from the University of Vermont and later his Ph.D. from Johns Hopkins University, Dewey began his academic career at the University of Michigan and concluded it at Columbia University. But it was his years at the University of Chicago that saw his thought reach maturity and his reputation established. Here he created his famous "Lab School," a living, self-correcting community as a testing ground for his evolving educational ideas. Here he emerged as one of the founders of that uniquely American brand of philosophy known as pragmatism.

Dewey was a prolific scholar, publishing scores of books and pamphlets, and hundreds of articles for scholarly and popular journals. He was the author of innumerable speeches and lectures on topics ranging from Hegelian metaphysics to women's suffrage. Dewey's works are often misunderstood, but as John Novak explains "Dewey is like the Bible—often alluded to but seldom read..."[26] Though he does not always write well, one must read Dewey to understand him. Key to this understanding is Dewey's response to the question: what is philosophy? Dewey resisted the conception of philosophy as "some sort of superscience," or "the foundational discipline of culture..." In different ways and in varying degrees, both the "implicative" and "applicative" views of educational philosophy embrace the Kantian notion of philosophy as foundational. Both approaches are wrongheaded because philosophy, for Dewey, is not a search for certainty, but an attempt "to gain critical perspective, to locate, specify, and clarify problems..."[27] Implicit in Dewey's vision is the idea that philosophy, in any meaningful sense, and education are one.

The key to understanding this intimate relationship between philosophy and education can be found in the term "philosophy" itself. Literally meaning the love of wisdom, Dewey explains that "whenever philosophy has been taken seriously, it has always been assumed that it signified achieving a wisdom which would influence the conduct of life."[28] Though facts may be helpful, wisdom moves beyond worldly facts to a general attitude or disposition about the world. Wisdom so defined is not a fixed entity which once found is to be routinely applied to all of life's questions, but a disposition or habit of seeking and creating connections among the disparate aspects of life. Philosophy, viewed in this way, loses its elitism and professional status. As Dewey explains "any person who is open-minded and sensitive to new perceptions, and who has concentration in connecting them has, in so far, a philosophic disposition."[29]

Dewey's philosopher is a critic, but more than criticism is needed. For example, in *The Public and Its Problems*, Dewey joins Walter Lippman in criticizing voter ignorancy and apathy, but Dewey goes further by offering a vision of what democracy can and should be. The problem, suggests Dewey, lies not in an inherent weakness of democracy or human nature, but in the failure of our institutions to promote democracy. Suggesting that such weak democracies stem from our founding fathers rather limited vision of what democracy could or should be, Dewey moves beyond the analysis of the past to suggest ways of transforming these weak or thin democracies into genuine or strong democracies.

As individuals become human, as they learn that communities are experimental and that they can and should contribute to their development or demise, the seeds of democracy are planted. To aid in this development of genuine democracy, that is, to assist every individual in learning how to become human, is the moral, political, and educational task of philosophy. As such, the major problem for the philosopher is communication, that is, making possible for the public at large to "acquire knowledge of those conditions that have created it and how those conditions affect the values of associated life."[30] If democracy is to survive and improve, progress must be made not only in the presentation of new knowledge as it is discovered and created, but also in the process of inquiry that lead to the creation and/or discovery of this new knowledge. To Dewey, the philosopher is not the expert who frames and executes policy but the wise amateur capable of assisting the development and dissemination of the procedures through which the masses can frame and execute policy. Fostering this kind of wisdom or intelligence is or should be the goal of all philosophers, especially educational philosophers.

The Dewey chapter concludes with a warning against reifying Dewey's vision into *the* educational philosophy and with the suggestion that we approach Lipman's claim that Philosophy for Children "is the only valid representative of Dewey's education put into practice" with skepticism. As explained in chapter 7, Matthew Lipman has struggled for more than twenty years to make philosophy more accessible by turning it inside out. In developing philosophical novels for and about children and youth, Lipman has implemented the Deweyian principles that "presentation is fundamentally important" and that democracy begins in the "neighborly community."[31] The result is the Philosophy for Children program which combines the pedagogical and dialectical aspects of philosophy.

Harry Stottlemeier's Discovery was Lipman's first attempt to dramatize philosophy so as to make it accessible to children and youth. Though Lipman's ideas about dramatizing philosophy have evolved in the almost quarter of a century since he wrote *Harry*, one can still find in this work the essential ideas found in all of the Philosophy for Children materials. Lipman has improved in his struggle to master the craft of dramatizing philosophy, but "Harry's" persistent struggle to figure things out—in Bruner's terms, "to go beyond the information given"—is a thread that permeates all of the Philosophy for Children materials. A fictitious fifth grader caught in the act of daydreaming in class, Harry attempts to reason himself out of a predicament. Experiencing embarrassment as a result of his failure, he turns his reasoning inward and tries to figure out his mistake. Through such reflection, along with a little help from his friends, he begins to unravel the mysteries of thought and subsequently to apply his discoveries to his everyday world. In *Harry* and in other novels written for and about children, Lipman offers children and youth an essentially Deweyian model of how to think.

Common to all the Philosophy for Children material is the goal of transforming the classroom into a self-corrective community of inquiry. Key to such a transformation is the appropriate use of dialogue as a teaching strategy. While Lipman acknowledges his indebtedness to Dewey, he takes this emphasis on dialogue from Socrates. Socrates, as portrayed in the dialogues of Plato, personifies the role that philosophy should play in our lives. In these dialogues, Socrates provides us with an excellent model of how discovery and understanding are enhanced through dialogue. In emulation of these Socratic dialogues, Lipman has developed stories, told from a child or youth's point of view, to dramatize the content and skills of philosophy. To the extent that students connect with the characters in the novels and their problems, they can be encouraged to discuss the philosophical dimensions embodied in these characters and problems. In the process, students contribute to the creation of a community of inquiry in their classrooms.

Lipman has devoted the past third of his life to turning philosophy inside out and to restoring its natural connection to education. Rather than considering philosophy the capstone or culminating discipline in the educational hierarchy, philosophy, suggests Lipman, is best suited to serve as introductory discipline for it prepares students to think in the other disciplines.[32] Philosophy dramatized can serve as a model, demonstrating for other fields of study how to dramatize themselves. Such dramatization is necessary if philosophy is to do what Dewey suggests it should do, that is, deal with the problems of humankind. In dramatizing philosophy, Lipman has provided us with an important, albeit imperfect model for reconstructing educational philosophy. It is perhaps the ultimate irony that an individual who purportedly trusts neither philosophers nor educators has shown us how philosophy can make peace with education.

In suggesting that those of us involved in the Philosophy for Children movement guard against reifying this approach or becoming a disciple of Lipman, the conclusion to chapter 7 anticipates the theme of the final and eighth chapter, "Educational Philosophy: Discipleship or Pilgrimage?" Once the philosopher embraces a particular system or approach as the one correct perspective, that person ceases to be a philosopher. For philosophy, including educational philosophy, to flourish, it needs to reconceptualize itself as a pilgrimage that is never consummated, rather than as the fountain of knowledge from which only a few are allowed to drink.

Traditionally, one of the roles of the philosopher is to develop conceptual schemes that seemingly "knit the disparate...tag end of things into clear and consistent wholes..."[33] While this quest for a unifying schema or theory is understandable, even commendable, a problem occurs when the products of such a quest are reified. Whenever an individual or group believe that such an ultimate unifying scheme has been discovered or developed, the philosophic quest ends and dogma, discipleship, and authoritarianism begins.

Contrast this to the philosopher as pilgrim. It is the rare individual who chooses the faith of the pilgrim, a faith characterized by "the commitment to the unending quest in which one's way is enlightened by all systems of thought but not fully directed by any one of them." Such a faith leads "not to an ultimate dogma but to wisdom."[34] With such wisdom comes a kind of humility for "in a state of wisdom (the pilgrim) discovers that, in all his knowledge, he does not finally know."[35]

If philosophers are to be more like pilgrims than disciples, the question becomes: is it possible to develop a defensible moral vision without that vision evolving into a domineering and imposing dogma or metanarrative? The ideas of such contemporary thinkers as Cornel West, David Purpel, and the late Kenneth Benne suggest than a moral vision grounded in process rather than in some foundational metanarrative is both possible and desirable.[36]

The issues revolving around what West labels prophetic thought are not new. They are similar to what John E. Smith characterizes as "America's Philosophical Vision." Although it manifests itself in a variety of ways, the overarching theme permeating this vision is the uniquely American emphasis on "the promise of the future over the significance of the past."[37] For a variety of historical, political, and geographic reasons, the many cultures that comprise what is known today as the United States have generally been concerned with what tomorrow will bring than what happened in the past.

Smith considers the American philosophical vision to be largely a pragmatic one, and prophetic thought as conceptualized by West, Purpel, and Benne is compatible with this pragmatic perspective. While some may challenge this perspective as a too narrow characterization of the American philosophical spirit, it is the perspective that is being advocated in this work. At its best, the Philosophy for Children program exemplifies this spirit and other exemplars of this prophetic perspective are discussed in this chapter.

Much of the final chapter, indeed much of this entire work, criticizes the past and present state of educational philosophy. While it is clear that field is not healthy, educational philosophers cannot afford to wallow in pessimism. Educational philosophers need to realize that their field is in jeopardy, but we must not lose hope for, to paraphrase Cornel West, the future is not preordained. While it is not possible for anyone to offer a sure cure for what ails the field, the purpose of this work is to encourage educational philosophers to embrace the prophetic vision that many of their mentors rejected earlier in this century. What we need is not more disciples of Dewey, but serious students of his thought who extend, reconstruct, and apply Dewey's insights in light of the educational and social problems facing humankind today. What we need is more of the kind of scholarship that the recent works of Gerald Grant and Nicholas Burbules exemplify.[38]

In facilitating the emergence of a hopeful vision of what Hamilton High could and should be, Grant exemplifies the prophetic thought of West and others. In helping others to develop a positive vision of the future, Grant exemplifies public philosophy in the Deweyian tradition. In contributing to the creation of a better world at Hamilton High and in analyzing the factors that contributed to such a creation, Grant provides us with a model of educational philosophy worthy of emulation. In his work, as in that of Burbules, the process or dialogue is emphasized. In this sense these two exemplary cases of scholarship in educational philosophy illustrate what is meant by the philosopher as pilgrim. While both Grant and Burbules demonstrate a commitment to a vision of what should be, theirs is a faith in dialogue as a process or processes that enable humankind to create and recreate their worlds. Such a vision allows, even compels one to act, but the process is a self-corrective one that must never be reified.

In keeping with West's fourth element of prophetic thought, I choose to conclude this work on an optimistic note. The field of education is at a crossroads. In its present form, it will likely fade away, or, at best survive as a relatively marginalized discipline in the modern university. For it to fulfill its potential and become an imaginative and integrative discipline contributing to the development of educational leaders committed to creating and sustaining strong democracy, educational philosophers need to follow the lead of Lipman, Burbules, and Grant and return to Dewey's prophetic vision as the starting point for reconstructing the field.

As Rugg suggested more than four decades ago, educational philosophers must be liberally educated but vocationally oriented. Educational philosophers must reorient themselves more toward the schools than the university if they are to satisfy their reason to be. As educational philosophers, along with our colleagues in the other social foundations of education, our "primary reason-for-being," as Steve Tozer explains, "is vocational preparation and development."[39] Perhaps it is the ultimate irony that for educational philosophy to achieve its potential and fulfill its reason to be, that is, to take a leadership role in developing teaching into an honorable profession, it must abandon its efforts to become a distinctive and academic discipline. For this to occur, those of us in the field need to think of educational philosophy, not as philosophy *of* education nor as philosophy *and* education, but as philosophy *as* education.

2

Nineteenth Century Origins
of Educational Philosophy

The nineteenth century origins of educational philosophy are complex and multifaceted. These roots are deeper and far more complex than is suggested by Kaminsky's claim, described in the introduction, that educational philosophy as we know it began with the establishment of The John Dewey Society at the Hotel Traymore in Atlantic City on Sunday, February 24, 1935. In investigating these origins, the linkages between philosophy proper and one of its "offspring" must be examined, but educational philosophy is not just a subset or branch of the larger field. A search for its origins also leads to the disintegration of the old moral philosophy course during the age of the university and to the relationship between the social reform movements of the late nineteenth century and the emerging social sciences.

At this point the skeptic might ask, what good is it to know or understand how these deep and complex origins coalesced to form educational philosophy? What does it matter? It matters, argues J. J. Chambliss, because "the study of its (educational philosophy) origins might be suggestive in determining not only what the philosophy of education has been, but also what it now is and what it might become."[1] This admonition, written by Chambliss in 1968, seems even more relevant today as educational philosophy struggles for its very survival as an academic discipline. In an attempt to both illuminate the current status of educational philosophy and to suggest how it should develop, an account of the origins of American educational philosophy is offered below. Our discussion begins with a brief overview of the nineteenth century "foundations" for this twentieth century academic discipline.

NINETEENTH CENTURY FOUNDATIONS OF EDUCATIONAL PHILOSOPHY

According to J. J. Chambliss, "it was not until the (late) nineteenth century that the philosophy of education was recognized as a distinct discipline."[2] Chambliss suggests that the writings of the inductive empiricists, rationalists, and naturalistic empiricists provide a small body of literature which indicates that by 1913 the discipline of educational philosophy was firmly established in the minds of serious students of education. By examining the nineteenth century origins of this emerging field, the intent is to increase our understanding, not only of what educational philosophy has been or currently is, but what it might become. With this in mind, a brief discussion of each of these three nineteenth century "educational philosophies" is offered. Particular emphasis is given to themes or ideas that remain current or controversial and which offer insights into what educational philosophy could have been and should be.

Inductive Empiricism

Early nineteenth century empiricists came close to making a metaphysics out of experience. These empiricists were absolutists, who believed that experience was the best guide to lead us to the absolute truths. Adopting and adapting the Baconian inductive method, the argument that "principles, rules, laws are found in inductions from one's own experience..."[3] is common to the inductive empiricists writing on education in the first half of the nineteenth century. According to these empiricists, Baconian induction is a natural process, "the kind of activity in which men would be engaged, if they allowed themselves to turn away from domination by a few already established arts, and turn towards the 'clear light of nature,' which illuminates the pathways of inquiry,..."[4] The intent of this emphasis on nature was to bring philosophy down from the clouds; to bring it down "to the level of the most ordinary abilities...," to open up a new and easy path upon "which not only the learned, but the studious and inquisitive in every rank of society, might walk with safety and success."[5]

This tendency to democratize philosophy produced, in the 1830s, some remarkably modern sounding educational ideas. For example, Horace Mann's legislative colleague James G. Carter suggests that students should not be given or told the rules that define the universe. Rather, by beginning with what is familiar and comprehensible, students should learn how to discover and make their own rules. Carter believed that by employing the Baconian method of induction as an instructional strategy, students would gradually reconstruct their own rules until they discovered the naturally best or absolutely correct rules that govern the universe. As we shall see this belief in a rational, orderly universe had its roots in the seventeenth century, but of interest here is the recognition that students must be actively involved in their own education. Such a perspective is reminiscent of subsequent and contemporary, progressive educational ideas.

Before turning our attention to the contributions of the rationalists to nineteenth century educational philosophy, it should be noted that the inductive empiricists were acutely concerned about the relationship between philosophy and education. For example, G. E. Partridge suggests that philosophy must be brought to bear on the concrete practical concerns of education. In this regard Partridge anticipates the admonition of Broudy and Price, among others, who lamented in the 1950s that there was not enough philosophy in the philosophy of education. Partridge also warns us of the dangers of "deriving the principles of education from systems of philosophy." Writing in the early 1900s, Partridge argues for "a more intimate relation between philosophy and education..."[6] Such themes merit our attention and we will return to them in subsequent chapters as we attempt to reconstruct the relationship between philosophy and education into philosophy *as* education. Also discussed later in this chapter are those inductive empiricists known as common sense realists who dominated American higher education for more than a hundred years in the eighteenth and nineteenth centuries. Their Scottish realism dominated the moral philosophy course taught to college seniors; a course that dealt with many of the issues and questions that the social scientists and educational philosophers struggle with today.

Rationalism

If, as is suggested above, the inductive empiricists reify experience, the rationalist look to reason as the means to arrive at the absolute. One can find both considerable agreement among rationalists and inductive empiricists regarding ultimate objectives or ends, and major disagreements over the means of attaining those ends. The rationalists argued that, through human reason, the work begun by the inductive empiricists could be completed; that is, human reason could "make known the 'invisible whole' from which came the fragmentary experiences of the sciences."[7] These rationalists, or speculative idealists, were most influential during the closing decades of the nineteenth century, winning widespread recognition for philosophy's role in both academic and public life. The great rationalist philosophers "were the spokesmen for philosophy in the grand manner and they taught as men having authority."[8] This authority was based upon speculative insight into the nature of ultimate reality, which in turn, "was the reward and rationally warranted outcome of the cumulatively successful inquiry in which philosophers for more two thousand years had been engaging..."[9] Such individuals, including those focusing on educational questions, achieved preeminence, not due to the clarity and soundness of their dialectical arguments, but for their sound judgement and vision combined with their ability to communicate such a vision to general audiences. Many of their students and some of their colleagues had trouble following or understanding their sophisticated dialectical arguments, but these philosophers assumed the mantle of judge and critic of all human learning, including science and theology. While there is much to criticize in this tradition, including its authoritarianism and elitism, the rationalists' ability to communicate their visions to a larger, nonacademic, nonprofessional audience is worthy of our emulation as we seek to reconstruct educational philosophy into philosophy *as* education.

For the first two-thirds of the nineteenth century, Scottish realism (inductive empiricism) and speculative idealism (rationalism) struggled for dominance as *the* philosophy to be taught in American higher education. For much of this period, the college reflected the values of a predominantly agrarian way of life. As the dominant form of higher education in America, the college served a "community of settled ways and ancient certainties."[10] While these philosophies permeated the college experience, their formal articulation took place in the senior course in moral philosophy—the course, from 1700 to 1850, serving as "the semisecular way station between the great era of theological dominance" of the Middle Ages and the twentieth century, "when objective science presses so hard on all other modes of experience."[11]

Naturalistic Empiricism

Naturalistic empiricism, more commonly known as pragmatism, objected to the reification of either experience or reason. Rejecting both idealist and realist absolutes, the naturalistic empiricists "argued that man's 'moral sense' needed no metaphysical cause." Chauncey Wright, writing a generation before John Dewey, suggests that neither experience nor reason can lead us to ultimate meaning. According to Wright, "meanings come, if at all, to individuals, and no particular subject matters will guarantee higher knowledge."[12] Dewey builds upon these ideas to suggest that no philosophical tradition can determine ahead of time the educational significance of a particular event or subject. Dewey warns of the danger in forcing the facts of education to conform to a philosophy already formed. Dewey is concerned with the tendency to think of education as dependent upon and derivative of philosophy in general. It is because of this concern that he develops a vision of educational philosophy that is best captured by his statement that "philosophy is, in its ultimate extent, a general theory of education."[13] Dewey's vision of the connection between philosophy and education is developed more fully in subsequent chapters. For now, it is enough to suggest that this vision combines the democratizing aspects of the inductive empiricists with the rationalists' ability to articulate a public vision into a new synthesis which offers clues for reconstructing educational philosophy into philosophy *as* education.

One can find in each of these three "educational philosophies" elements of a new synthesis—of what is referred to by contemporary writers as philosophy *as* education.[14] Philosophy as education is appropriately associated with Dewey and other pragmatists, but as West and others have argued, the roots for such a synthesis can be found in the thought of Ralph Waldo Emerson. Often associated with the transcendentalists and thus with rationalism, Emerson eludes such labelling by refusing to "swim in a regulated pool nor allow others to imitate his stroke."[15]

Not a philosopher in the traditional sense,

> Emerson viewed knowledge not as a set of representations to be justified, grounded, or privileged but rather as instrumental effects of human will as it is guided by human interest, which are in turn produced by transactions with other humans and nature.[16]

To Dewey, Emerson was not just a philosopher but a poet creating truth "in the sonnet and the play."[17] He was more than a philosopher in that he was "a maker rather than a reflector," a seer or prophet rather than just a critic of his world and society. In opposing "creed and system, convention and institution, Emerson," as Dewey explains,

> stands for restoring to the common man which in the name of religion, of philosophy, of art, and of morality, has been embezzled from the common store and appropriated to sec-

tarian and class use. Beyond any one we know of, Emerson has comprehended and declared how such malversation makes truth decline from its simplicity, and in becoming partial and owned, become a puzzle of and trick for theologian, metaphysician and litterateur—a puzzle of imposed law, of an unwished for and refused goodness, of a romantic ideal gleaming only from afar, and a trick of manipular skill, of specializing performance.[18]

In suggesting "that philosophy is still rude and elementary; it will one day be taught by poets,"[19] Emerson anticipates the work of Rorty and other postmodernists. If, as is suggested here, Emerson provides us with a uniquely American vision of what philosophy could and should be, the question becomes why has his evasion of philosophy only recently become of interest. Why, for all practical purposes, were his ideas on what philosophy could and should be largely ignored during much of the nineteenth and twentieth centuries? In terms of our focus, why did educational philosophy, as it emerged as an academic field of study alongside the social sciences, deny the Emersonian vision of what philosophy could and should be? In an attempt to respond to such questions, we turn now to a discussion of the "old time" college's capstone course in moral philosophy. This course, usually taught by college presidents, not only enabled inductive empiricists, rationalists, and—to a lesser extent—naturalistic empiricists, to shape the character of the future leaders of the nineteenth century; but also gave birth to the modern social sciences and influenced the character of what would soon become educational philosophy.[20]

THE OLD MORAL PHILOSOPHY COURSE

With the emergence of moral philosophy, circa 1750, as the capstone course for college seniors, the American college succeeded in unifying the classical curriculum and in developing the moral character of its students. These dual purposes, grounded in an essentially Christian world view and later undergirded by the Scottish common sense philosophy, dominated American higher education for more than a century. Presenting philosophy as the unifying science of all knowledge, the old moral philosophy course offered students a unified world view, and by stressing Christian ethics, sought to develop their moral character.

Though often referred to as the "Queen of the Sciences," the moral philosophy course has rarely been the subject of serious study.[21] Even the famous Yale Report of 1828 makes only passing reference to the senior course in moral philosophy. In response to critics opposed to the retention of the "dead languages" in the curriculum, the Report eloquently defends the classics as being "especially adapted to form the taste and discipline the mind, both in thought and diction, to the relish of what is elevated, chaste, and simple,"[22] but offers no apologies for moral philosophy.

Perhaps there was no need to defend the moral philosophy course as apparently reformers and classicists alike recognized its importance. Even Francis Wayland, an early advocate of the elective principle, "made moral philosophy ... in his new system, the only subject required of all degree students."[23] As president of Brown University from 1827 to 1855, Wayland used this harmonious blend of theology, social science, and Christian ethics to unify both a narrow classical curriculum and studies of a more practical nature.

George P. Schmidt described the course as infusing a "breadth of intellectual life... into the dead body of the college,"[24] and the course was generally acclaimed as the most popular science in the curriculum. Defined as "the science that teaches men their duty and their reasons for it,"[25] the moral philosophy course aimed at assisting young men in distinguishing right from wrong and at illustrating, through reason and revelation, the inherent unity of all knowledge.

These common ideals formed the skeleton for the course, but each individual instructor, usually the college president—drawing from his own background, ability, and education—added sinew. Content and emphasis differed from college to college and changed with time. The most significant change occurred near the end of the eighteenth century as the Scottish common sense realism, introduced to American colleges by John Witherspoon of the College of New Jersey, gradually replaced William Paley's theological utilitarianism as the dominant system of thought taught in the course. The principal difference between this Lockean philosophy of sensationalism and that of the Scottish "naive" realism was the latter's belief in a moral sense. According to the Scottish realists, just as every individual possesses a common or mental sense through which descriptive ontological truths can be intuitively grasped, each individual's moral sense enables him or her to intuitively grasp prescriptive, ethical truths. Just as mathematics and the classics were especially suited for disciplining the mind or mental faculty, moral philosophy served the equally important role of disciplining the moral faculty.[26]

During the latter half of the nineteenth century, both the Christian world view and the Scottish common sense philosophy encountered serious challenges. Darwin's *Origin of the Species* was particularly harmful to the "argument from design so popular in college philosophy,"[27] and Scottish realism gradually gave way to the more historically oriented philosophies such as German idealism or some version of American pragmatism. In short the theoretical and philosophical underpinnings of the old moral philosophy course no longer satisfied the needs of an increasingly urban, industrial society. The German emphasis on research, the demand of a growing industrial society for more practical knowledge, and an essentially elitist demand for liberal culture surfaced as rivals to the more traditional aims of a collegiate education. All of these factors contributed to the disintegration of the moral philosophy course as the university emerged as the dominant form of higher education in America.

PHILOSOPHY IN THE AGE OF THE UNIVERSITY

A revolution occurred during the last thirty years of the nineteenth century transforming both the purpose and structure of American higher education. The elective principle, the German ideal of pure research, the clamor for a more utilitarian education, all coalesced to produce radical changes in American higher education. The end product was a unique institution, as the American university emerged to replace the "old time" college as the dominant form of higher education in America. The emergence of this new institution is associated with the rise of modern science. Together they transformed the curriculum of American higher education.

Though travelling in opposite directions, the emerging university and the declining moral philosophy course were moving on parallel tracks. As the new social sciences (political science, economics, sociology, etc.) emerged out of the remnants of this capstone course, there was some doubt whether philosophy, as a field of study, could survive in this new, scientifically oriented university. As the new social sciences struggled to legitimize themselves by establishing professional journals and associations for the purpose of articulating and expanding the specialized and increasingly scientific knowledge base of their fields, philosophy confronted similar yet different problems. Philosophy had been the "queen of the sciences" since the Middle Ages, but it no longer occupied a privileged position in the curriculum. Issues and questions that had previously been the exclusive domain of philosophy were now being investigated scientifically by historians and other humanists as well as by social scientists. Confronted with the possible demise of philosophy as a separate and distinct field of study, philosophers gradually and reluctantly chose to emulate other academic disciplines and took steps to establish their field of study into another academic discipline.

Philosophers differed from the new social scientists in that they sought "to restore the authority and legitimacy philosophy once enjoyed and to partake of the strength and prestige that seemed to accrue to the more highly organized disciplines."[28] The professionalization of philosophy and educational philosophy is the subject of a subsequent chapter, but illustrative examples of philosophy's fate during this period are offered here to help us better understand how and why educational philosophy developed as it did.

In order to survive and prosper in this new university structure, the academic department took on an added significance. The modern American university was and is a hierarchical institution consisting of a board of trustees, a president or chancellor, deans, and department chairs, followed by several gradation of faculty members.[29] For most faculty and students, the organizational unit that most affected them was the department. This structural unit, while not new, took on added significance within the university as the elective principle and the emphasis on research required that knowledge be organized into precise fields of study. As the university ideals began to dominate American higher education, the department emerged as a semiautonomous entity in the major universities during the 1880s and 1890s.[30] In many of these institutions, department chairmen became men of great importance. Some ruled their departments as dictators and almost all struggled to expand their department's size and prestige within their university and in comparison with similar departments in other institutions.

Critics suggested that this trend toward departmentalization and specialization made the mind "microscopic in vision and minute in method, rather than truly comprehensive and penetrating."[31] Such criticism was not entirely unfounded, but there were positive as well as negative results to the growth and development of the departmental structure. A case in point was the department of philosophy at Harvard in the late nineteenth century. While the departmental structure often enabled faculty members to function as semiautonomous individuals, the structure facilitated Harvard's faculty in philosophy functioning as a group.

This smooth functioning, yet diverse unit became the envy of other academic departments, then and now. Part of its success can be attributed to the skill of the senior member of the department in handling the routine affairs "smoothly and reasonable."[32] Though a lesser light philosophically than James, Royce, or Santayana, George Herbert Palmer's contribution as the department chair should not be underestimated. Through his efforts, the great talents of the department were allowed the freedom to pursue their individual projects with a minimum of interruptions for departmental business. Combine this with Palmer's ability to orchestrate the natural disagreements among members as "a friendly, not a hostile process,"[33] and you have an outstanding administrator. By creating an atmosphere where individual members felt comfortable in openly disagreeing or criticizing one another, the department fostered a kind of intellectual dialogue that brought out the best of these exceptionally talented and diverse individuals. Rather than degenerating into jealousy, "anger, factionalism, and disorder," a rare exhilarating atmosphere had been created that enabled "all the academic potentialities... to be realized."[34]

Created here was one of those rare communities of inquiry that characterizes philosophy at its very best. Here diversity was courted and teaching was emphasized. In building the department, members consciously sought individuals with different philosophical orientations than their own. The philosophy department at Harvard championed no school of thought, but, believing that the surest way to approaching the truth was through criticism, sought talented thinkers from diverse philosophical perspectives. The department expected each member to speak his mind and encouraged them to share these thoughts with students. The department emphasized teaching and each faculty member took his turn in teaching or team teaching large undergraduate survey courses. In short, the late nineteenth century philosophy department at Harvard, by creating a genuine community of inquiry and inviting their students to participate in it, approximated the ideal of what philosophy could and should be.

What happened in Harvard's late nineteenth-century philosophy department was and is rare. The old moral philosophy course was little more than a memory in Harvard's grand philosophy department, but vestiges of it were clearly visible in other institutions. As the name suggests, the old moral philosophy focused on moral instruction, but what happened to the teaching of ethics with the demise of this course? An examination of this question is illustrative for, as Douglas Sloan argues, "a look at the teaching of ethics provides, as it were, a central window on the whole of American education."[35] A course entitled "moral philosophy" became increasingly rare during the decades following the Civil War, but the remains of this tradition were clearly visible well into the 1890s. For example, "in 1895, the Amherst College catalogue devoted the entire first page of the 'The Course of Study' to a description of the course in ethics taught by the president of the college to the senior class."[36] A decade later, there was no such emphasis on ethics in the catalogue, merely a course offering listed among several electives available for sophomores. This example of ethics becoming just another course at Amherst is illustrative of how far philosophy had fallen from its once lofty perch atop the undergraduate curriculum. That this could occur at Amherst and other liberal arts colleges—the self-proclaimed champions of a traditional college education—demonstrates the power and momentum of the forces coalescing to transform American higher education and creating the modern university.

In order to survive as a field of study, philosophy had become, by the early decades of the twentieth century, a professionalized and largely secularized discipline. Small liberal arts colleges, like Amherst, begrudgingly accepted the change as inevitable. Institutions founded during this period more willingly embraced the ideals of the university and welcomed the professionalization and secularization of the disciplines, old and new alike. For example, the treatment of philosophy at Cornell, founded as a university, offers an interesting contrast to the prominence instruction in philosophy played at numerous small colleges. With no long tradition to reconcile and financially opulent—due to the munificence of Ezra Cornell and as the beneficiary of the funds available to New York State from the first Morrill Act—Cornell readily adopted many of the ideals associated with the modern university. In the post-Civil War years, moral philosophy was still a significant offering at most colleges, but it never became an indispensable part of the curriculum at Cornell. As in the case at Amherst, presidents of many small colleges still offered instruction in moral philosophy or in one of its components. Andrew Dickson White, the co-founder and first president of Cornell University, lectured to the students in history, not moral philosophy. The registrar and general handyman, the Reverend William D. Wilson, served as Cornell's professor of mental and moral philosophy. Wilson represented the amateurism of an earlier age that was an unwelcome anomaly at Cornell in the 1870s and 1880s.[37]

In the mid-1880s Cornell's longtime friend and benefactor, Henry Sage, endowed a professorship in ethics and handpicked Jacob Gould Schurman as the first professorship of the Susan E. Linn Sage Professorship of Christian Ethics and Mental Philosophy. Sage endowed this professorship for the explicit purpose of securing for Cornell University "the services of a teacher who shall instruct students in mental philosophy and ethics from a definitely Christian standpoint."[38]

Sage's purpose in endowing a chair and later a school of philosophy is compatible with ideals embodied in the old moral philosophy course.

In contributing $200,000 for the establishment of a school of philosophy at Cornell, Sage sought to provide a complete education for all Cornell students, to include a "thorough cultivation of his moral religious side."[39] Cornell readily accepted Sage's gift and moved quickly to establish the school of philosophy, but the university obviously did not share Sage's essentially religious orientation. The school opened in 1891, with the stated purpose, as announced at the dedication, at variance with Henry Sage's original desires. The trustees hoped "to make this school a thoroughly efficient center for maintenance, diffusion, and increase of knowledge and activity in America."[40] The school proved to be a success eventually developing a laboratory and publishing a journal, but it is questionable if it ever served the expressed purpose of its benefactor.

The Cornell example illustrates the variance between traditional philosophy and the ideals of the modern university. At Cornell moral philosophy received only token recognition during the first fifteen years of the institution's existence. Jacob Schurman's instruction was a definite improvement, but most of his offerings, in addition to being electives, were more in tune with a secular liberal culture orientation than with antebellum moral philosophy. Without a heritage to restrain it, Cornell, when given the chance to develop a religiously oriented department of philosophy, created instead a secular, more scholarly enterprise.

The transformation of the study of philosophy from a broadly based humanistic and synthesizing discipline into a specialized and scientifically oriented field continued into the early decades of the twentieth century. As the cases of Amherst and Cornell suggest, there were conflicting perspectives on what philosophy's role in higher education ought to be. Should the issues traditionally discussed in college philosophy courses retain their focus on values or should these issues be subjected to the rigor and objectivity of science? As philosophy was struggling to define its role in this new science-oriented institution, the new fields of study spawned by the old moral philosophy course experienced many of the dilemmas of the parent discipline. As the fields of political science, economics, philosophical ethics, psychology, anthropology, sociology, and eventually educational philosophy began to distinguish themselves as separate and distinct fields of study, they "often carried with them the moral and ethical imperatives of moral philosophy."[41]

The first generation of social scientists achieving faculty status in the modern American university were public advocates for various social reforms. As they became imbued with the academic culture of the university, and as they struggled to achieve intellectual respectability for their own emerging field of study, these academics began, by the mid-1890s, to "dissociate themselves from reform causes, and to emphasize their devotion to scientific research and their professional ties." While sympathetic to the need for change, they "discovered...that their activities as popularizers and reform advocates—as ethics teachers to the nation at large—required precious time from their scholarly and scientific research."[42] Many social scientists sought to have it both ways in the closing decades of the nineteenth century, but eventually they "disengaged themselves from direct social action," and "their fields [became] increasingly dominated by a stress on scientific method as ethically neutral, on a scientific, objective, and quantitative understanding of social science research, and on tighter professional, organizational control."[43]

Of the initial social science disciplines emerging from the old moral philosophy course, sociology resisted the siren song of science longer than the others and retained its moral and ethical dimensions well into the twentieth century. Perhaps, as shall be discussed in subsequent chapters, this explains Dewey's favoring the study of sociology over professional philosophy for those wishing to use philosophy.

Thanks to the influence and vision of Albion Small, sociology seemed like a likely candidate to replace the old moral philosophy course "as the unifying science of the study of man..."[44] According to Small, "Sociology in its largest scope ,..., is merely a moral philosophy conscious of its task, and systematically pursuing knowledge of cause and effect within this process of moral evolution." "Science is sterile," suggests Small, "unless it contributes at last to knowledge of what is worth doing. The ultimate value of sociology as pure science will be its use as an index and a test and measure of what is worth doing."[45]

In spite of the best efforts of Small and others, sociology eventually joined the other social sciences in embracing the scientific ethos associated with the modern American university. Three years after the death of Small, William F. Ogburn's 1929 presidential address to the American Sociological Society clearly places sociology in the scientific orbit of the modern American university. According to Ogburn:

> Sociology as a science is not interested in making the world a better place in which to live, in encouraging beliefs, in spreading information, in dispensing news, in setting forth impressions of life, in leading the multitudes, or in guiding the ship of state. Science is interested directly in one thing only, to wit, discovering new knowledge.[46]

With sociology joining the other social sciences in embracing the dominant scientific ethos, the path for educational philosophy was clearly marked. The roots of educational philosophy as a field of study are closely associated with social sciences as they emerged during the latter half of the nineteenth century. With the most comprehensive of the social sciences—sociology—succumbing to the pressures of the scientific and professional ethos, it is not surprising that educational philosophy, despite valiant efforts to hold on to the moral and ethical dimensions of the old moral course, gradually became just another professionalized academic discipline.

THE SOCIAL SCIENCES AND EDUCATIONAL PHILOSOPHY

In discussing the origins of educational philosophy, it is not enough to search for the roots in social and moral philosophy. Obviously, such an explanation must include an examination of the linkages with the larger field of philosophy, but, in the case of educational philosophy, it must also include a discussion of the emergence of the social sciences and their relationships to the social reform movements of the late nineteenth century. As Kaminsky argues,

> ...understanding how social science—the discipline and the social movement—emerged from philosophy in the second half of the nineteenth century is crucial for understanding both educational thought and the philosophy of education, which emerged from one of social science's most active departments, education. Social science, education, and educational reform were related concepts in Europe and the United States in the middle of the nineteenth century, having a common ancestry in social and moral philosophy.[47]

During the later half of the nineteenth century, social science and social reform movements joined forces in an attempt to solve the problems brought on by the industrialization and urbanization occurring during this time. While the social problems associated with this watershed period of our history were enormous, there was a sense of optimism that these problems, through the power of ideas, could be resolved. This largely middle-class naiveté contributed to the establishment of the American Social Science Association in 1865 as an organization designed "to propose solutions to the social problems generated by industrialization and urbanization."[48] As a whole this Association exhibited tremendous faith in the power of education. Attributing the social ills accompanying industrialization and urbanization—drunkenness, prostitution, brutality, etc.—"to be a function of ignorance," "education seemed an elegant and economical solution to social problems."[49]

This rather naive faith in education as the panacea to the staggering social problems of the day manifested itself in the organization of the Association into four major departments: Education, Public Health, Social Economy, and Jurisprudence. In suggesting that the serious study of social institutions could yield information useful for solving the social ills of the day, the Association served as a kind of precursor to the development of the social sciences as legitimate fields of study in the emerging American university. With its emphasis on education, the Association formalized education's affiliation with the social sciences. While the relationship among and between these emerging scientific, social disciplines and education is both subtle and complex, it contributed to educational philosophy, along with various social sciences, finding its "way into U.S. universities."[50]

As already noted, these new academic fields of study emerged out of the old moral philosophy course of the eighteenth and nineteenth centuries. As Kaminsky suggests, the efforts toward creating a single or one social science discipline—as a more secular, scientific version of the old moral philosophy course—failed. Instead, various social science disciplines—sociology, education, political science, and economics—were established as distinct fields of study in American universities. As we have already seen, these new disciplines retained, at first, the moral and ethical dimensions associated with the old moral philosophy course. But, as the nineteenth century drew to a close, these new disciplines gradually abandoned their more liberal, social concerns "in the name of methodological purity."[51]

Educational philosophy as a field of study eventually followed suit, becoming just another professionalized field of study housed in the university. But as Kaminsky explains, this professionalization did not occur until well in the next century. For the remainder of the nineteenth and well into the twentieth centuries, educational philosophy struggled to retain its social and moral agenda. For a time, at least, it was possible to envision educational philosophy as the heir to the more liberal elements of the old moral philosophy course. At this time, it remained an open question whether educational philosophy would become another scientifically oriented and specialized field or fulfull its potential as an expansive, humanistic field of study concerned with developing teachers and others into leaders of an evolving society committed to democratic principles. This possibility has been all but lost, as educational philosophy—

like its parent discipline and the social sciences, including sociology—
rejected this uniquely American and Emersonian vision and became,
instead, an overly professionalized and largely irrelevant academic discipline. In the words of Harold Rugg, educational philosophy chose the
"conforming way" rather than the "creative path."

Educational Philosophers: Leaders or Followers of American Higher Education

During the late nineteenth century, a secularized and increasingly
professionalized philosophy survived and occasionally flourished in the
modern American university. As described above, Harvard's department
of philosophy served as the model of what academic philosophy could
and should be in the modern American university. In reality, this golden
age of philosophy at Harvard was short lived and few institutions were
able to effectively emulate it. Educational philosophy, as it emerged
between 1890 and 1920, failed to achieve the autonomy or freedom of
thought that characterized Harvard's department of philosophy. To the
extent that educational philosophy retained its ties to the old moral philosophy course, it embraced the conservative aspects of the course and
assumed a rather traditional stance in American higher education. By its
very nature, the old moral philosophy course represented the conservative
tradition of nineteenth century America. Given this it is not surprising
that educational philosophers and other academics responsible for improvising programs for the training of teachers in the university chose what
Harold Rugg calls the "conforming way."

While the bureaucratic structure of the modern university was well
established by the end of the nineteenth century, schools or colleges of
education in which departments of social foundations (including educational philosophy) were housed did not emerge as part of the university
until the opening decades of the twentieth century. Prior to the establishment of such schools or colleges, a few institutions included profes-
sorships in pedagogy, such as Harvard's Professorship of the History and
Art of Teaching and Columbia's Professorship of Philosophy and
Institutes of Education. In the years preceding and following the Civil
War, efforts were made to include instruction in pedagogy as part of the
curriculum in American higher education. As early as 1850, President
Wayland succeeded in establishing at Brown University courses in the
"science of education" and in "didactics."[52] Following the Civil War, the
University of Iowa finally succeeded in establishing a "Chair of Mental

Philosophy, Moral Philosophy, and Didactics." By the 1890s, departments of pedagogy had been established in several prominent universities, including Michigan, Indiana, Stanford, Illinois, and California. Still, it remained an open question whether instruction in educational philosophy belonged in these new departments of pedagogy or in departments of philosophy.

The dilemma over whether to emphasize its educational or philosophical dimensions has plagued educational philosophy throughout its brief history. Harold Rugg suggests that in choosing either side in this debate, the teachers of teachers in general and educational philosophers in particular embraced the status quo or what he calls the conforming way. Those responsible for developing university programs for the training of teachers tended, suggests Rugg, to listen to the advocates of the liberal arts tradition, or liberal culture as it came to be known in the age of the university. In combining the metaphysical conservatism associated with the old moral philosophy course with the protective structure of the bureaucratic university, those improvising programs for the training of teachers were able to develop a curriculum to train teachers that fostered traditional beliefs and values.

The individuals responsible for bringing teacher education and thus educational philosophy into the university had come of age during the latter half of the nineteenth century. Most had attended college during the "midst of the Darwinian controversy." These "founding fathers" of university teacher education embraced Darwins's theory of evolution, but their acceptance of it followed Herbert Spencer's interpretation of the theory rather than Dewey's or that of Darwin himself. From the writings of such influential education professors as Nicholas Murray Butler, Paul Monroe, William C. Bagley, Ernest N. Henderson, William C. Ruediger, Edward L. Thorndike, and George D. Strayer,"it is clear that evolution meant to them 'adjustment', 'adaptation'—that is conformity."[53] From the collective perspective of these prominent education professors, the purpose of education was to pass on to each new generation the best that the western world—presumably the best society to date—had to offer.

Of particular significance for the field of educational philosophy is the role that Nicholas Murray Butler played in the founding of Teachers College, Columbia University and in teaching educational philosophy there for more than a decade. As a young Columbia University Fellow in Philosophy, Butler began offering lectures for teachers on professional education on Saturday mornings in 1886. The popularity of these lectures contributed to the establishment of the New York College for the Training of Teachers in 1897, with Dr. Butler as its president. Eventually becoming Teachers College, Columbia University in 1892, Butler served as president only until 1890. At this point he became Dean of the Faculty and Professor of Philosophy and Education of Columbia University, but he retained his affiliation with Teachers College, creating and teaching "Principles of Education" there until he assumed the presidency of Columbia University some dozen years later.

Butler's "Principles of Education" was a course in educational philosophy, using Herman Harrel Horne's *Philosophy of Education* and Paul Hanus's *Educational Aims and Values* as texts. Also required reading was Butler's own work, *The Meaning of Education*, and works by Davidson covering ancient educational ideas; Eliot on educational reform; and Harris on educational psychology. The course as Butler developed it and as it was taught by his successors "abounded in generalities"; was largely "idealistic and Hegelian in philosophy"; and advocated "the scientific study of education."[54] Conceiving of education as "the adjustment of the individual to the world," this Teachers College graduate level course was representative of the field of educational philosophy from its development in the 1890s up to World War I.

In suggestion that ten of the fourteen educators identified as the founding fathers of the first foundations of education were affiliated with Teachers College, Rugg's assessment of the role Teachers College played in the shaping of teacher education and related fields is inflated.[55] The contributions of Teachers College and those affiliated with it are significant, but, more importantly, Rugg's basic point is on target. Those individuals and institutions responsible for the development of professional education in general and educational philosophy in particular were defenders of the status quo. The philosophers and educators involved in creating new disciplines and new professional programs thought of education as the transmission of a culture rather than as a critique of culture or as an attempt to rebuild it.

While many of these founding fathers were contemporaries of Dewey, Veblen, Beard, Boas, Robinson, and Turner, those in positions of influence, including Butler, chose the "conforming way" over the "creative path." Like the conformists, advocates of the creative path embraced Darwin's theory of evolution. To them, Darwin's notion of a universe with the lid off offered an opportunity for education to be more than just a means of adapting to an ever-changing world. Education could now become a process of recreating and rebuilding the world into a better place for all humankind. This more optimistic view—what some have labelled 'reform Darwinism'—characterized those advocating the creative path. But those capable of making a difference as the new field of educational philosophy was being established rejected this view. Apparently neither educators nor philosophers were ready for the creative path at the turn of the twentieth century. A generation later, the ideas associated with the creative path would, for a time, be seriously considered. As we shall see in the next chapter, this interest in the creative path is short-lived and the field of educational philosophy squandered another opportunity to become an expansive, integrative discipline. Instead, educational philosophy became by the mid-twentieth century just another specialized and professionalized academic discipline. In doing so educational philosophers became followers, rather than leaders, of American higher education.

3

Educational Philosophy in the Twentieth Century

Educational philosophy emerged as a distinct discipline during the first half of this century. Not surprisingly, its emergence as a field of study parallels the development of schools or colleges of education in the modern American university. During its formative years, indeed for much of its existence, educational philosophy assumed the role of a dependent child, looking to its parent, philosophy, for guidance and nurturing. During this nurturing phase, the developing field of educational philosophy progressed from an overreliance upon the 'isms' or systems approach to an infatuation with logical and linguistic analysis. The strengths and weaknesses of both of these approaches—identified here as the "implicative" and "applicative" views of educational philosophy—are detailed below, including a discussion of their pedagogical effectiveness. Noting that both approaches or traditions have made significant contributions to this emerging field, the chapter concludes by suggesting that neither is independent enough to lead the discipline to maturity.

PHILOSOPHY DURING THE TWENTIETH CENTURY

It is ironic but not surprising that, during its infancy, educational philosophy ignored John Dewey's warnings and mimicked its parent at a time when philosophy itself was experiencing an identity crisis. The fate of the parent discipline remained in doubt as philosophers argued among themselves over what role they could and should play in the university and in society. A few diehard rationalists continued to insist that philosophy was still the queen of the sciences, but whether these claims came from

> mathematical logicians who, like Russell, and the early Wittgenstein, sought to derive from a study of elementary calculus of propositions an ontological map which charts the essential forms of 'facts', or neo-Thomistic apologist for the 'perennial philosophy' of their medieval master,[1]

most philosophers recognized that the queen of the sciences metaphor had been seriously challenged during the seventeenth century and effectively debunked by Hume and others during the eighteenth and nineteenth centuries.

As Barrett and others suggest, philosophy in the twentieth century is perhaps best described as a revolt against classical rationalism, particularly as expressed in the idealism of Plato. Put simply, idealism represents the tendency to place essence over existence. In Plato's case, essence meant eternal, transcendent ideas, but Bertrand Russell transformed essence to mean the truth of mathematical or logical propositions. By focusing on the mathematical and logical aspects of philosophy, Russell and others sought to retain philosophy's role as a foundational discipline if not the queen of the sciences. Russell and others, by suggesting that the ultimate keys to reality could be found in the disciplines of logic and mathematics, proclaimed *the* philosophical method for unlocking the mysteries of reality. Perhaps unwittingly they embraced the Platonic legacy while simultaneously rejecting its more intuitive elements.[2] Later in this chapter, the impact of the belief that there is one correct, or *the* philosophical method or approach on educational philosophy is discussed.

The twentieth century revolt against idealism took many forms, often resulting in philosophers arguing among themselves about the very nature of their discipline or field of study. The cleavage between the British and Continental philosophical orientations is illustrative of this debate. Barrett suggests that the difference between them can "be stated as one between analysis and intuition."[3] Barrett further explains that the Continental philosopher will, after study and reflection, try to explain what he or she has learned or knows and thinks about the problem under investigation. The British philosopher "presents himself in the act of unraveling his reasons, chipping away at words and sentences, even when the reasons may lead to only a goat's worth of conclusion."[4] This latter technique may be useful for graduate students as it undoubtedly helps sharpen their mental acumen, but it also runs the risk of creating "philosophers" whose first reaction to anything new or unfamiliar is to consider it intellectually soft or meaningless. This risk is significant for it precludes or denies a sense of openness that is essential to the philosophic enterprise.

The trends described above, including the decline of speculative idealism, were well underway by the end of World War I. In parallel fashion the significance of American pragmatism was on the rise, but it failed to achieve philosophical dominance in either academic or public forums. As Arthur E. Murphy tells us, the period between the two world wars might properly be called the "age of isms."[5] With idealism on the wane and pragmatism unable to replace it as the dominant philosophical tradition, the academic study of philosophy focused temporarily on a comparative study of the "isms." A typical "Introduction to Philosophy" course in the twenties and thirties would expose students to the standard "isms," presenting the positions taken by each system and offering criticism of these positions. The instructor's preference or philosophical orientation, though usually not announced, could often be determined by the discriminating student.

With the "isms" dominating academic philosophy in general, educational philosophy followed suit. When done well, the "isms" approach is a legitimate way of doing philosophy, but it was not always done well, particularly when those not well trained in philosophy began teaching educational philosophy. Many academic philosophers were unwilling or unable to demonstrate philosophy's worth to future educational professionals. For this reason, as schools or colleges of education emerged as part of the modern university and for the purpose of professionalizing the field, they began to prepare "their own specialists in the psychology, history, and philosophy of education—recruiting in most instances, their experts in these fields from among their own or other schools of education, not from academic departments."[6] The result was, as Broudy and others would soon suggest, not enough philosophy in the philosophy of education.

PHILOSOPHY OF EDUCATION: THE IMPLICATIVE VIEW

During the first half of the twentieth century educational philosophers and the courses they taught usually focused on one or more "ism" and can be grouped into one of the following three types. The first is the least important for it was falling out of favor during the 1930s and 1940s.

This type was a carry over from the nineteenth century as these educational philosophers identified with and advocated a particular system or approach. Books published and classes taught by these educational philosophers generally meant an introduction into the philosophy of the author or instructor. If the authors or instructors were skilled in conveying not only their position but the reasons undergirding it, some students undoubtedly caught the philosophical spirit from such philosophers. But, since most prospective educators took at best only one course in the philosophy of education, discipleship, rather than genuine philosophical understanding, was often the result. John S. Brubacher criticized this type of educational philosophy as fostering a kind of educational astigmatism, best corrected through the comparative study of educational philosophies.[7]

This brings us to the second type of educational philosopher prevalent during the first half of this century. Much like the "Introduction to Philosophy" course described earlier, many educational philosophers taught courses and published texts, during the 40s, 50s, 60s, and even 70s, introducing students to various and often competing philosophical systems or "isms." Such courses or texts often began by explaining these larger philosophical traditions' response to questions of reality, knowledge, and goodness, moving deductively to a discussion of such educational theories as essentialism, perennialism, or progressivism. As already noted, Dewey and others warned of pitfalls associated with this approach, but it is not without its merits. This approach is often criticized for not *doing philosophy*, but it need not be this way. As Harry S. Broudy argues, if it is done well, one can *do* philosophy using this approach to the same degree one can *do* philosophy using other approaches.[8]

There remains the danger, identified by Dewey and others, that such a system runs the risk of forcing educational practices to conform to *a prior* philosophical systems. Such a danger can be minimized, if not eliminated, by introducing these philosophical systems as explanatory hypotheses and inferring from them possible educational practices. For such an approach to avoid the pitfalls identified above, the focus must be on explaining how things could or might be rather than how they must be. The time may be ripe to revive this largely debunked "isms" approach in modern form for it appeals to the practitioner who can readily identify certain associations between the particular beliefs of a particular system and what goes on in the classroom. Such an approach, especially if it provides a historical context for the examination of various "isms," is particularly valuable as the first or only course in educational philosophy that the student is taking. Whether such an approach is effective in encouraging and empowering practitioners to be more thoughtful and reflective professional educators is dependent to a large degree on the skill and knowledge of the philosopher teaching the course or courses in educational philosophy. We will return to this topic in a later section and discuss its pedagogical and curriculum implications.

The third type of approach to the teaching of educational philosophy is often referred to as the "great minds" approach. This is a variation of the "isms" approach discussed above, and while it has been frequently used in this country, it was more widely used in Great Britain. In much the same way that the "isms" were taught, the beliefs of the great thinkers regarding the question of reality, knowledge, and value were studied and the implications for educational practice inferred. The great minds approach is subject to many of the same criticisms leveled at the comparative "isms" approach. In addition, as our world becomes increasingly pluralistic, the selection of which great minds to include becomes increasingly problematic. While efforts have been made in recent years to include non-Western selections in the anthologies developed as text materials for use in teaching the "great minds," there remains a tendency to focus on the educational ideas of the great thinkers of western civilization. This approach seems particularly susceptible to gender criticism, since the focus is almost always on ideas of great men in what has been male dominated cultures. In addition, just as there is a danger of overgeneralizing in regard to the basic tenets of certain systems of thought, there is a danger here of not treating great minds in sufficient depth to develop an understanding of their contribution to and relevance for contemporary education. Whether such an approach can assist educators in understanding and appreciating philosophy's worth to their profession, and whether such an approach can overcome its history of cultural and gender bias, is dependent upon the knowledge, perspective, and skill of the individual writing the text or teaching the course.

These three types of educational philosophy dominated the field until midcentury and they are still prevalent in many less research-oriented institutions. Giarelli and Chambliss characterize these three types as the "implicative" view or the "philosophic positions" view of educational philosophy. They explain that from this perspective, "the activities of educational philosophy are derived from philosophy."[9] As such this kind of educational philosophy seeks to serve two masters; the community of academic philosophers on the one hand and the community of practicing educators on the other. From this perspective educational philosophers are in the middle "translating and transmitting the foundational knowledge required to ground the realm of educational practice."[10] In short this is philosophy *of* education.

John S. Brubacher, Professor of the History and Philosophy of Education at Yale University, championed this comparative approach as the corrective for the professional astigmatism resulting from a too narrow view of educational philosophy. As chairman of the National Society for the Study of Education's Committee on Philosophies of Education, Brubacher is largely responsible for presenting the field as a study of philosophical "isms" and their implications for educational practice in the first yearbook devoted to educational philosophy. Appearing in 1942 and titled *Philosophies of Education*, the 41st NSSE Yearbook discussed the educational implications of five major systems of thought. A chapter is devoted to each "ism" or system with each author presenting the ultimate reasons "for carrying on the educative process as they... believe it should be carried on."[11] In the final chapter Brubacher compares and contrasts the "isms" so as to enable both experienced and inexperienced teachers to understand the efficacy of each system in solving specific educational problems or issues. No attempt, Brubacher suggests, is made in determining which, if any, of these philosophies students should accept or which, if any, is *the* philosophy of education.

Brubacher champions this comparative approach but not without reservation. Obviously influenced by Mortimer Adler's argument in an earlier chapter of the yearbook that "there is only one true philosophy of education, only one body of philosophical knowledge about education, and not a variety of equally entertainable 'systems', ..."[12] Brubacher seemingly agrees that the discussion of conflicts over philosophical and educational matters must take place within a common frame of reference. Though Brubacher rejects Adler's Aristotelianism as *the* philosophy of education, he seeks to reduce conflicts and wonders "how can such a common frame of reference be agreed upon?"[13] If there can be no agreement, what role, if any, can educational philosophers play in helping students and/or teachers to choose among the several competing positions? More importantly, what role should educational philosophers play in influencing such choices? Brubacher finds himself in a quandary. Seeking unity but no longer willing to accept Aristotelian or other metaphysical absolutes, the only plausible option seems to be to enlighten students regarding the several educational positions or "isms" available to them and let them choose. Brubacher's solution effectively means that the educational philosopher has little or no responsibility for guiding the largely moral choice students make in selecting which system or "ism" to embrace.

Brubacher continues to champion this approach, presenting it once again in slightly altered form in the second NSSE yearbook devoted to educational philosophy. Still, as the title of the 54th yearbook (*Modern*

Philosophies and Education) suggests, change was in the air. While Brubacher was still seeking unity or *the* philosophy of education, many educational philosophers had found it, not in the Aristotelianism of Adler, but in a positivistic science and the methodology of logical and linguistic analysis. Taking its cues from Russell and others during the early days of this century, philosophy in general moved rapidly in this direction following World War II. Educational philosophy would soon follow suit.

PHILOSOPHY AND EDUCATION: THE APPLICATIVE VIEW

The "isms" approach clearly dominates the 54th NSSE yearbook, but "real," rather than educational philosophers, were asked to write the chapters explaining and extolling the virtues of the various systems. To ensure relevance, an educational philosopher was paired with each of the authors. Still, the limited contribution made by the most prominent educational philosophers to this prestigious publication is indicative of the increasing awareness that the philosophy of education needed more philosophy. One such contributor to the 54th NSSE yearbook, Harry Broudy, an educational philosopher from Framingham State Teachers College, continued this call for more philosophy in the philosophy of education in his very influential "How Philosophical Can Philosophy of Education Be?" paper which appeared in the October 27, 1955 issue of the *Journal of Philosophy*. Not surprisingly, Broudy suggests that educational philosophy should be more philosophical, arguing that "the philosophy of education in the hands of both educators and philosophers boils down to a set of general and not very illuminating statements about the good life and what, in the light of their experiences and preferences, the schools ought to be doing about it. Such a body of assertions and exhortations does no particular harm, but it scarcely qualifies as an academic discipline, and certainly not as a philosophical one." Broudy goes on to note that courses in philosophy of education exist in many institutions, but those teaching them "cannot even by courtesy be called philosophers or philosophers of education."[14] To remedy this deficiency, Broudy suggests that candidates for higher degrees in philosophy of education need professional training in both philosophy and education. Furthermore, he argues that graduate students in philosophy need not worry that by entering the realm of educational philosophy that they are abandoning philosophy. According to Broudy "one cannot leave philosophy and still be a philosopher of education."[15]

Broudy's article, along with one accompanying it (Kingsley Price's "Is a Philosophy of Education Necessary?"), had an immediate and significant impact. In response to the questions raised in these two papers, the *Harvard Educational Review* published a special issue the following spring devoted to the purpose and scope of educational philosophy. Distinguished philosophers and philosophers of education contributed to this volume, and many were critical of the "isms" approach. Overall, there was general agreement with Broudy's admonition that educational philosophers needed more training in philosophy. Broudy, while aware of the weaknesses of the "ism" approach did not abandon it completely. But, with philosophy in general embracing logical and linguistic analysis as *the* philosophical method, Broudy's call for more philosophy in the philosophy of education contributed to this still embryonic discipline shifting "its attention to the logical and linguistic analysis of educational concepts and problems."[16]

In hopes of attaining greater academic credibility, the "implicative" view or philosophic positions approach to educational philosophy gave way to the "applicative" or analytic view. From this perspective, educational philosophers were to do more than study about the philosophic positions of others. Instead they were to *do* philosophy. This meant applying the tools of analytic philosophy to problems and issues of education. In short, this meant a "strong emphasis on analysis, both logical and linguistic, entailing considerable attention to the problems of ambiguity and vagueness, definition, claims, slogans, metaphors, and formal and informal fallacies of reasoning."[17] As Jonas Soltis explains, educational philosophy from this perspective is a narrower, more technical and more professional discipline concerned with the more modest role of identifying and correcting conceptual and linguistic mistakes.

At its worst this kind of educational philosophy became the new scholasticism, trivializing educational issues by engaging in medieval-like disputations over clarity, inconsequential distinctions, and insignificant presuppositions. Particularly disconcerting here is the all too common practice of "making conceptual points by means of deliberately trivial examples."[18] While this is done to prevent the linguistic or logical point being made from being lost in the emotions and prejudices surrounding genuine issues, it is disconcerting to see real problems "degenerating into criteria for the grading of apples, or even for assessing sewage effluent."[19]

Despite these weaknesses, this kind of educational philosophy has made significant contributions to the field. A case in point is the work of the British analytic philosopher, R. S. Peters. Peters is well known for his work on the nature of motivation and education as a form of initiation, but his contribution is more than just linguistic and/or logical analysis. Peters brought to these issues and to all of his work "considerable knowledge of psychology,...experience of a variety of educational institutions and his extensive knowledge of the history of philosophy."[20]

Peters himself is critical of the analytic movement for it "brought with it a rather narrow, piecemeal approach." Not only is it lacking an explicit theory of human nature, but "conceptual analysis has tended to be too self-contained an exercise."[21] Peters explains that a criteria for a concept cannot be found in the usage of the term alone. The term must be understood in both its historical and social context or the conceptual analysis must be related to some genuine educational problem. Philosophers like Peters added substantial knowledge and experience to this linguistic and logical approach to educational philosophy, but not all engaged in analysis brought such knowledge and experience to the task. Obviously, the "applicative" approach to educational philosophy has much to offer when it is done well. But when it is done poorly, scholasticism, not increased understanding, is the result.

In 1981 the third NSSE yearbook devoted to educational philosophy appeared.[22] Much like its predecessors, this more recent yearbook attempted to both illustrate what educational philosophers do and the relevance of their activity to the educational practitioner. Those responsible for this latest yearbook, most notably Jonas Soltis, acknowledge the chasm separating the professional philosopher from the practitioner, but suggest that the chasm results from the practitioner's rather narrow view of what educational philosophy is or should be. While agreeing that the educational philosopher needs to do a better job of demonstrating the connections between philosophy and education, the emphasis remains on employing or applying the techniques of philosophy to educational issues or problems. Each of the chapters comprising this 80th NSSE yearbook were written by active educational philosophers, but their topics were consciously drawn "from the way in which philosophy in general is ordered in colleges and universities today, namely by means of its subfields of philosophical inquiry..."[23] To its credit the yearbook includes chapters on curriculum theory, a theory of teaching , aesthetics, moral education, and critical thinking as highly trained specialists connect these subfields of philosophy to education. While these efforts are commendable and reflect the evolving multifaceted nature of the field, as the title suggests—*Philosophy and Education*—the applicative view of educational philosophy is still dominant in the 80th NSSE yearbook.

The analytical school's dominance of educational philosophy since midcentury has been a mixed blessing. Undoubtedly there is more philosophy in educational philosophy than was the case in 1950, but the emerging discipline has not freed itself from its dependency upon philosophy in general. As Giarelli explains, educational philosophers remain subservient to the parent discipline, not by explaining the implications of philosophical truths for educational practice, but "as a kind of technical support staff which uses the techniques of professional philosophy to bring some consistency to the muddled realm of educational discourse."[24] Perhaps this is a legitimate role for the educational philosopher to play, but all too often the analytic educational philosopher has been unable or unwilling to communicate to the practitioner how this brand of educational philosophy is useful and meaningful to those working in schools and other educational institutions. For this reason, educational philosophers no longer have a public outside of the university and professional educators no longer look to them for guidance.

PEDAGOGICAL IMPLICATIONS OF THESE TWO APPROACHES

To many contemporary philosophers, the "implicative" or systems approach to educational philosophy represents, at best, the history of philosophy rather than the act of philosophizing itself. From this perspective those engaged in the systems or "isms" approach are not *doing* philosophy and hence are not true philosophers. The suggestion that the "isms" or systems approach to the study of educational philosophy is not genuine philosophy denies my own introduction to the field of educational philosophy, and it runs counter to my own experience teaching educational philosophy for more than a decade.

Through undergraduate courses in the social foundations of education, I was aware of educational philosophy as a field of study, but my first substantive encounter with it occurred during my first year of graduate study. Professor Jack Conrad Willers taught this introductory course in educational philosophy and used G. Max Wingo's *Philosophies of Education: An Introduction*. Though not aware of it at the time, Willers and Wingo introduced me to both the content and methodology of the field. Wingo's text provided a solid foundation in the basic schools of philosophical thought and their implication for educational practice. Professor Willers's love of wisdom was contagious, and he personified the detailed analysis of ideas and persistent sense of wonder that characterizes genuine philosophy. Whether a masters level student taking this course to fulfill a degree requirement or a serious student of the field (as I considered myself to be), Professor Willers used Wingo's text as a springboard for stimulating our thinking on things of importance to each of us. While Willers's gift for engaging us in the philosophic enterprise cannot be overemphasized, equally significant was his use of Wingo's text. On the first day of class he suggested that we read Wingo over the weekend, thereby freeing up the rest of the semester for more interesting reading. As a naive graduate student, I thought he was serious. By the next class meeting, I had read all 356 pages of the text. I did not understand much of what I had read, but by rereading the text as the semester progressed, my understanding of the field deepened. Under Professor Willers's guidance, I also read deeply into the primary literature, using Wingo's text as a guide to the many mysteries that educational philosophy presented for me.

If my experience as described above is a legitimate case of 'doing philosophy', the question remains to what extent can this be attributed to the text or to the instructor. Was it Willers or Wingo that transformed the course into a philosophical experience? Professor Willers's contribution to my development as an educational philosopher is significant, but my experience is not typical. Most of the students enrolled in Professor Willers's 1974 class had never taken and would never take such a course again. For me, the text may not have been critical, but after teaching graduate level educational philosophy courses for more than a decade, I have become increasingly aware of the importance of appropriate text material. Like my classmates in Willers's introductory educational philosophy course, most of my students had never taken a course in philosophy or educational philosophy, and never took another one.

What is it about Wingo's text that distinguishes it as an outstanding introduction to the field of educational philosophy? What is it about a text originally published in 1965 and revised in 1974 that remains a powerful introduction to the field for both the serious and not so serious student of educational philosophy? According to Wingo, a student confronting a field as diverse and complex as educational philosophy "needs something to help him fit together the things he reads, the ideas he hears in lectures, and the practices he observes in schools."[25] In short, students need a conceptual or organizational framework that enables them to meaningfully question this new (to them) and mysterious field. As Wingo suggests, the intent of the text is not to provide students with *the* answers but to enable them to understand the basic questions of the field and to stimulate investigation into issues or problems that may be introduced or treated superficially in the text. A good text will, suggests Wingo, enable and encourage the students to inquire further into the field, that is, to investigate key questions and problems as they relate to issues of significance to them.

Much of the previous discussion offers good advice about text material in general, but what is it about Wingo's text in educational philosophy that distinguishes it from others? The answer is simple. While Wingo recognizes that, like mathematics, educational philosophy can be studied with little or no attention to its implication for practice, he employs philosophy in an attempt to help students to understand contemporary educational practice in the United States. For this reason, he chose an approach that seeks to "construct a comprehensive view of educational activity *in its social context*."[26] Much like Brubacher before him, Wingo eschews indoctrination, but his text is more than just a comparative study of the "isms" and their implications for education. He does provide students with a detailed historical and philosophical analysis of five major philosophical traditions influencing contemporary education, but his approach is thematic and offers a historical and contextual dialogue among and between these five traditions.

Wingo takes as his point of reference the widely held view that "the purposes the American school has generally served are those of preserving and transmitting the so-called essentials of Western culture and of acting as a conserving, civilizing force in society."[27] As he accurately explains, these purposes are reflected in the way schools are organized and what and how students are taught. Wingo begins with a detailed analysis of the conservative tradition, followed by a discussion of its implication for education. After a lengthy explanation of the philosophical foundations and problems associated with such educational conservatism, Wingo introduces the reader to four distinct and often warring protests against conservative educational thought. These four traditions span the philosophical spectrum, but they share a common opposition to this dominant conservative tradition in education. Wingo analyzes each of these traditions as a historical body of thought that at differing times and for differing cultural reasons mounted a serious challenge to the conservative tradition's hegemony over education.

Not everyone embraces Wingo's thesis that conservatism is the dominant tradition in American education. Not all agree with his analysis of educational essentialism and the liberal, perennial, Marxist, and existential protests of it. These are, at best, but one way of framing the study of educational philosophy. Wingo's interpretation is not offered here as the true, or best way of studying educational philosophy, but to suggest that the use of conflicting and competitive views of education's role in society is an effective way of introducing students to both the historical struggles that partially define the field and to the methods of analysis various traditions have used to confront these struggles.

To the extent that these struggles transcend cultural and temporal boundaries, students connect these struggles to issues that concern them personally. In this way, students begin to emulate, not mimic, the various educational philosophers or traditions and begin to understand that their questions and problems as thinking human beings are often very similar to those addressed within these larger traditions. In the hands of a skilled and knowledgeable instructor, the Wingo text and others like it enable students to come to grips with the philosophical presuppositions undergirding particular traditions in education and involves them in a dialogue with past and present thinkers concerned with the crucial problems of education. In short, by presenting educational philosophy as an evolving, never-ending conversation, the Wingo text makes educational philosophy accessible to students.

Intuitively, both as a student and teacher of educational philosophy, the Wingo approach made sense to me, but why? A partial answer to that question is provided in Kieran Egan's *Teaching as Story Telling*. In this little book, Egan is largely concerned with teaching and curriculum design for young children, but what he offers is applicable to the manner philosophy is taught and learned.

Egan suggests that not enough attention is given to the role imagination plays in education, noting that educational psychology, sociology, and philosophy largely ignore it. Instead of imagination, the modern world has embraced a set of what Egan identifies as ad hoc principles which continue to "have a pervasive and profound influence on teaching practice and curriculum design." According to these principles education proceeds "from the concrete to the abstract, from the simple to the complex, from the known to the unknown, from active manipulation to symbolic conceptualization."[28] Perhaps unwittingly, we have accepted these principles since they are grounded in a logico-mathematical perspective of our world and because of our society's tacit acceptance of a seventeenth century concept of knowledge. As Egan notes, our dominant model of curriculum building and lesson planning coheres with a view of knowledge as a static entity, thus denying or minimizing imagination's role in the education process.

Egan offers numerous counter-examples, not to debunk these ad hoc principles, but to suggest that they are not always the best way and that they do not encompass the totality of education. To balance the widely accepted dictum that "Children learn best from concrete, hands-ons experiences," Egan explains that much of the literature for young

children depends upon the child's prior understanding of various underlying, but abstract concepts. Using the story of Cinderella to illustrate his
point, Egan notes that five year old children have no trouble understanding and enjoying this story though such understanding is dependent
on their ability to grasp such abstract and conflicting concepts as fear/
hope, kindness/cruelty, and good/evil.

Egan offers other examples drawn from children's literature to
refute the position that "abstract concepts in general are difficult for
young children."[29] Egan suggests that "seeing the process of education as
a development from the concrete to the abstract is a result of focusing on
certain limited logical intellectual activities."[30] The problem here is that
the education of young children has been reduced to almost total reliance
upon these ad hoc principles. In a similar fashion, as twentieth century
philosophy embraced logical and linguistic analysis, the result was to
reduce the social and affective dimensions of philosophy.

Egan's argument is important for it suggests that children possess
sophisticated conceptual tools at a much younger age than the ad hoc
principles allow. Their ability to make sense of rather complex fantasy stories suggests that children have the conceptual tools necessary to deal
with abstract subjects as history and philosophy. As Egan suggests one
learning procedure that can be observed in children "is the dialectical
process of forming opposites and mediating between them. For example,
in learning the temperature continuum, children tend to learn binary
opposite concepts of 'hot' and 'cold'. Next they mediate between these
and learn the concept 'warm.'"[31]

It is at this point that Egan's argument contributes to understanding how and why the Wingo approach to the study and teaching of educational philosophy has been so effective. Like Egan's young child, the
student using Wingo's text encounters increasingly complex variations of
the conservative-liberal binary opposite. By introducing students to educational essentialism and its challengers, students are encouraged to use
their imagination to find or create the contextual meaning of these historical conceptual frameworks. In short, students are encouraged to join
in the conversation between these binary opposites and use them to assess
their own views of these perspectives and to begin to construct their own
hues of gray by mediating between these two extremes. It has been suggested that such a process is a fundamental characteristic of all human
learning. Whether this is true or not, it is clearly an appropriate approach
to use in the teaching and study of educational philosophy.

Students relate to this approach because it enables them to participate in creating a meaningful story of educational philosophy. As Egan

suggests, "telling a story is a way of establishing meaning."[32] The Wingo approach introduces students to an incomplete and never-ending story of educational philosophy and invites them to join in the continuous development of it. It is a story, not in the fictional sense, but more like an editor asking a journalist "for an account of the particular events imbedded in some abstract context which readers (in this case students) already understand."[33] From this perspective, educational philosophy becomes a way of establishing and creating meaning in the educational process.

If the "isms" approach, as modified by Wingo, focuses on meaning, the analytic approach, as described by Jonas Soltis in his *An Introduction to the Analysis of Educational Concepts*, emphasizes clarity. Soltis suggests that for anyone to genuinely understand the various "isms" or schools of educational philosophy, they must first be introduced to the tools of analysis. Such an introduction should "whet the appetite and provide skills for further and more intimate contact with a field of study."[34] At least for Soltis, it is not a question of either the analytic or "ism" approach but whether a study of the tools of analysis should precede the study of the great minds and traditions.

Soltis contends that most teachers, as well as students, "would be hard pressed to spell out in simple words the ideas contained in such ordinary concepts of education as teaching, learning or subject matter."[35] Arguing that understanding such concepts is basic to any meaningful discussion of education, Soltis believes that such grounding is essential if the nuances of meaning in these terms as used by the great minds and traditions are to be unveiled. Soltis is convinced that mastery of the tools of linguistic analysis not only makes our collective use of these terms become more sophisticated, but also results in greater "insight into education as a human endeavor." "This," proclaims Soltis, "is the point of the philosophical analysis of educational concepts."[36]

Analysis of educational concepts is an important and worthy objective, but must such analysis precede the introduction of the great minds or traditions of educational thought? Cannot the tools of linguistic analysis be honed by comparing and contrasting the meaning associated with these concepts by various individuals and traditions? The claim that philosophical analysis needs to precede the study of the 'isms' is akin to the claim that children learn best by proceeding from the concrete to the abstract, from the simple to the complex, and from the known to the unknown. Just as the widespread acceptance of these ad hoc principles has reduced the role that imagination plays in the education of children, the overemphasis placed upon linguistic and logical analysis by many analytic philosophers denies the social and affective dimensions of educational thought.

As Soltis explains, the analytic approach puts clarity over commitment.[37] Using the tools of analysis, educational philosophers seek to hold their values at bay while examining the logical features of particular educational ideas. By breaking down each concept into its component parts, it is assumed that the 'truth' or essence of that idea can be attained. In short, analytic educational philosophers emulate the value-neutral techniques of the social scientists in their attempt to discover the true or most accurate meaning of a concept or term.

In a footnote, Soltis recognizes that this value-neutral stance is a luxury available only to academic philosophers. The practicing educator cannot remain neutral.[38] Such neutrality may be useful in attaining clarity, but only in terms of a limited scientific world view embraced by advocates of the analytic approach. The analytic approach is not value-neutral, but dependent upon and derivative of a particular and somewhat limited scientific view of the world. Clear thinking is a worthy educational goal, but an overemphasis on linguistic and logical analysis resulted in a sanitized version of educational philosophy. In the process, many educational philosophers became technicians in love first and foremost with precision and clarity. Unfortunately, such philosophers often failed to take the next step of translating or applying such precision and clarity to the messy and imprecise world of human action. This failure to effectively guide or inform the educational practitioner has reduced analytic educational philosophers to communicating among a decreasing number of like-minded individuals. As David Purpel and others have suggested, educational philosophers have lost their soul, precipitating a moral and spiritual crisis in educational thought.

Soltis is an advocate of the analytic approach, but he does not deny the value of other approaches. Noting that philosophizing can be done well or poorly using either the analytic or "isms" approach, it is telling that Soltis uses a metaphor drawn from science to compare the two approaches. He suggests that using analysis is like using a microscope, while employing the traditional world view approach is akin to using a telescope. Continuing the metaphor, each is designed to perform different tasks, but each has value and in certain situations can and should compliment one another. Still, from Soltis's perspective analysis is basic and should precede even a comparative study of the traditional educational world views.

Soltis and others conceptualize the field of educational philosophy as hierarchical, with analysis providing the foundation upon which all else rests. The view presented here suggests that good educational philosophy is much more complex and dynamic than a hierarchical structure allows. As Clive Beck explains, "Good philosophy of education has always been—because it must be—a complex of world view theorizing, careful analysis, medium-range problem solving, subtle interpretation, respectful dialogue, and many other things beside."[39] To those who suggest that educational philosophers should "clarify and criticize, and let others recommend," Beck notes that "we cannot clarify and criticize except from a base of substantive commitment."[40] For educational philosophy to achieve its full potential, it must abandon this hierarchical and specialized conceptualization of the field. Rather than withdrawing into the sometimes arcane world of specialized conceptual analysis, educational philosophers need to establish new forms of communication and collaboration.

Rather than isolating ourselves by speaking and writing only to one another, we need to establish new ways of cooperating and communicating with different and larger audiences. We must find more common ground with our colleagues in schools and colleges of education, and we must reach out as equals to those that our philosophizing is supposed to benefit. For that to happen, the field of educational philosophy must abandon the road toward professionalism taken by its parent discipline. The siren song that led educational philosophy down that path toward professionalism is the subject of the next chapter, with subsequent chapters examining various remedies to professionalism.

4

The Professionalization of Philosophy and Educational Philosophy

In this century, suggests Russell Jacoby, "full-time professors with their own organizations and journals replaced the lawyers, librarians, and scientists, the "relatively free intelligentsia,' who once constituted American philosophy."[1] Both philosophy in general and educational philosophy in particular joined other academic disciplines moving down the path toward professionalization. In our attempt to understand the past, present, and future of educational philosophy, it is important to know why and how this happened to the most expansive of all disciplines. Bruce Wilshire, William Barrett, and others suggest that professionalization of all fields, including philosophy, became inevitable when the modern American university chose to organize itself around a seventeenth century conception of knowledge. The legacy of this Cartesian perspective and its relationship to the United States culture of professionalism provide the focus for this chapter. In this context, the role that both the American Philosophical Association and the Philosophy of Education Society played in professionalizing philosophy and educational philosophy is discussed. To further illustrate the efficacy of this twentieth century drive toward professionalism, the transformation of the John Dewey Society from an association formed to foster radical reform into another, rather typical professional society is explained. The chapter concludes by suggesting a new mission for educational philosophy and by noting the irony that in fulfilling that mission, educational philosophy must abandon its desire to become a professionalized field of study.

SPECIALIZATION AND PROFESSIONALIZATION: THE CARTESIAN LEGACY

The seventeenth century was, suggests William Barrett, a strange century "which begot our modern epoch."[2] During this century a "new science" was created which, in turn, ushered in the modern world. Though this "new science" eventually supplanted religion to become the metaphysics of the modern world, its creators were deeply religious men. The greatest of these—Kepler, Galileo, and Newton—were fascinated by what they believed to be the mechanical nature of the universe. The distinctiveness of this "new science" was its emphasis on experimentation, particularly experimentation that involved the construction of machines. In their minds, nature itself was a machine subject to universal laws and principles that could be discovered by careful and persistent experimentation. Though the creators were not fully aware of it, the "new science" was as much the product of their own mathematical abstractions as it was of empirical experimentation. In short, this mechanistic world view was as much invented as discovered. As Barrett notes, "the presence of mind is everywhere in the formation of this science, and yet the results of this science were to be alleged as evidence for some general mechanistic view of the world, according to which the human mind appears as feeble and unfree."[3]

These contradictions became apparent to later generations, but the founders of this "new science" remained unaware of a possible collision between traditional religious views and this mechanistic view of the universe. To them, such a rational system served as evidence of a rational universe created, if not managed, by a rational god. Whitehead would later label this mechanistic perspective as "scientific materialism," and Barrett suggests that this scientific materialism "was to become *de facto* the dominant mentality of the West in the three and a half centuries that followed."[4]

The paradox between the religious perspective of the creators of this "new science" and its inherent naturalism, while interesting, is not our focus here. Our concern is in detailing how this mechanistic view of the universe produced both the specialization and fragmentation of knowledge and the professionalization of the disciplines. Once this general process is explained, the particular cases of philosophy and educational philosophy are discussed.

While Copernicus, Kepler, Galileo, and Newton were significantly responsible for the discovery and invention of the mechanistic perspective known as "scientific materialism," it is the philosopher, Descartes, a proselytizer for this "new science," who incorporated it into a larger philosophic vision. Living at a time when Copernicus's theory of a sun-centered universe caused one to question the knowledge derived from the senses, Descartes (1596–1650) tackles the problem head-on. The "new science" may cause human beings to doubt their senses, but they cannot doubt their own consciousness. It must be there in order to be deceived. Or as Barrett explains, "if I doubt the existence of my own consciousness, the doubt itself is a conscious act. So the ego comes back upon itself in its own unshakable world."[5] From this perspective the self or mind takes precedence over objects of the external world. The mind is now superior to and extracted from its world. The result of such a process is the isolation of the self or mind from the rest of the world. How then are the self and world connected? In an attempt to reunite the mind to its external realities, Descartes reasons that as an imperfect being, one's conception of a Perfect Being could only come from such a Perfect Being itself. This Perfect Being, or God, must be good, since goodness is a characteristic of this Perfect Being.

As Barrett explains, one more step is needed for Descartes to solve this epistemological problem of the self separated from its world. "Since God is good, he would not have created our minds so that they are deceived about the world around them. If we use our faculties properly, we can have valid knowledge of the external world."[6] The result is a partitioning of minds and bodies, which eventually, and perhaps unintentionally, feeds "a materialism in which only natural science is credited with powers of truth, and ethical and aesthetic judgments are construed as merely the expression of feeling and preferences of self as private ego."

As A. N. Whitehead notes, the twentieth century university developed according to the principles of this "new science" and Cartesian thought. The result is a division of the world into material bodies and weightless minds. As the university (particularly the American university) embraced these principles knowledge became "fractured into sciences and humanities, with only the former thought to deliver objective meaning and truth." According to Whitehead, "the revolutionary physics of our century, with its repercussions for reconceiving self and world and for integrating fields of learning, came too late to be incorporated in its [the university] structure."[8]

This Cartesian view of knowledge and the knower also contributes to the drive toward professionalization that characterizes most modern fields of study. Viewed from this seventeenth century scientific perspective, the universe is seen as a mechanistic entity, external to humans. It is further assumed that by a careful, rigorous, scientific examination of the universe, humans can discover and/or unravel the mysteries of nature. Doing this means applying the methods of science to an ever increasing number of specialized fields of knowledge. Presumably, by adding up the fruits of such specialized labors, an understanding of the whole is achieved. Emerging in the closing decades of the last century, the modern American university organized itself in accordance with this Cartesian view of knowledge. This, in turn, contributed to the specialization and professionalization of academic disciplines as the divisions of knowledge follow "inexorably and rapidly" from "the broad outlines of Cartesian psycho/physical assumptions."[9]

Many of the technological advances we enjoy today came about due, in part, to such specialization, but at a cost. As a consequence of this drive toward specialization and professionalization, the ability and desire to reach a common understanding of basic concepts shared by all disciplines has all but disappeared. Such isolationism and fragmentation of knowledge is compounded by another assumption suggesting that only in the university can one find knowledge of the universe as it really is or actually functions. According to Wilshire, knowledge derived from outside the university or from the talented amateur is suspect. This, in turn, has resulted in the bestowing of virtual metaphysical authority upon the scientifically trained specialist, especially if that expert is sanctioned as a professional by the university. These issues are developed more fully in the sections that follow.

PROFESSIONALISM AND THE AMERICAN UNIVERSITY

As noted above, one of the consequences of the Cartesian dualistic world view was the segregation of the mind from the body and the use of the "new science" to search for the principles or laws that supposedly define and govern each. As Wilshire and Barrett argue, this denies individuals the opportunity to discover or create meaning through coming to know and understand their surroundings, past and present. In addition to alienating the self, this Cartesian legacy undermined the more integrative institutions which humankind had historically used (church, family, school, community) to find and create meaning in their lives.

Such threats to traditional institutions occurred throughout the Western world, but with more immediate and dramatic effects in the United States. In a nation formed, in part, in rebellion against many of the traditions of the Old World, the legacy of Descartes proved to be unusually powerful. In the United States as elsewhere, people felt the need to distinguish themselves one from another. In more traditional societies this need was met by title, by ownership of property, by military rank, or by religion, but none of these were acceptable in this new, experimental, democratic republic. The frustration created by this unfulfilled need grew during the nineteenth century as the group that today we call the middle class emerged. In response to this need the modern world in general, and the United States in particular, turned to professionalism as the means to distinguish between individuals and groups without relying on tradition or barriers common in Europe and other more traditional societies. As the visiting James Bryce observed: "In a country where there is not titled class, no landed class, no military class, the chief distinction which popular sentiment can lay hold of as raising one set of persons above another is the character of their occupations, the degree of culture it implies, the extent it gives them an honorable prominence."[10] Americans, perhaps more so than any other modern society, embraced professionalism for it allowed them to establish an identity and find meaning in their lives without connecting to a particular community or tradition.

As Wilshire points out, one of our strongest needs is to "locate ourselves somehow within a *world*."[11] Since the more traditional ways of *being* within such traditional institutions as the family, the church, or the monarchy were no longer available to nineteenth-century Americans, they embraced professionalism as the modern-day answer to the perennial problem of belonging. This trend was clearly visible by the 1860s. In place of a more traditional basis for order, middle-class Americans sought to replace it with professional basis for institutional order. Evidence of this trend is seen in the growing dissatisfaction with the versatile amateur. Amateur, "which earlier in the eighteenth century had simply referred to a person who pursued an activity for the love of it," took on an increasingly negative connotation as the nineteenth century progressed. "*Amateurish*, a mid-nineteenth century word, connoted faulty and deficient work, perhaps defective, unskilled, superficial, desultory, less than a serious commitment, the pursuit of an activity for amusement and distraction."[12] Compare this to the eighteenth century connotation of the word 'amateur.' At that time, to be an amateur philosopher meant to pursue wisdom for the love of it. As we will soon see, such an "amateurish" pursuit of wisdom was not good enough for philosophers and educational philosophers affiliated with the emerging American university.

The move toward professionalism swept the United States in the late nineteenth century. No vocation or occupation was immune as middle-class Americans aspired to upgrade their occupational status. Even undertakers severed their ties with gravediggers, cabinetmakers, livery-men, and makers of funeral furniture. Emerging professional vocabularies demarcate the layman from the "professional," as ordinary coffins became caskets, cemeteries became memorial gardens, shrouds gave way to slumber robes. In an attempt to appear professional and in command of a special knowledge and skill, language often became inflated as "a decaying corpse became a 'patient' prepared in an 'operating room' by an 'embalming surgeon' and visited in a 'funeral home' before being laid to rest in a 'memorial park.'"[13] By developing a special language, supposedly shared only by experts, the profession or aspiring profession created, in many cases, a bogus authority for those practicing the "profession." While this example of the mortician and mortuary science is both humorous and extreme, similar efforts were made by both philosophers and educational philosophers during the nineteenth and twentieth centuries as they struggled for respectability for their respective fields in the modern American university.

The move toward professionalism and the development of the modern American university were complementary movements. As the American middle class embraced professionalism as the replacement for the "jack of all trades" amateur, they looked to the university as the appropriate vehicle for training and credentialing these new, scientific experts. As the nineteenth century progressed, a professional came to mean someone possessing specialized, scientific knowledge of a particular field or vocation, that is, a professional transcends mechanical procedures, anecdotal evidence, and knowledge gained by trial and error, and attains an understanding of the underlying principles and theoretical rules of the discipline or field.[14] Attaining mastery of the complex, theoretical underpinnings of a field or vocation was not easy, but those willing to focus their energies on ever increasing areas of specialization could achieve high status and financial reward. Herein lies the Cartesian legacy. The belief that by a proper use of their mental faculties, selected human beings could come to accurately and completely know the external world resulted in focusing attention on increasingly specialized fields of study as aspiring professionals sought scientific knowledge of such fields and subfields.

This growing middle-class faith in professionalism provided Americans with a new form of authority. Lacking or rejecting traditional forms of authority, middle-class Americans readily embraced science as their new metaphysics. Professionals, armed with scientific knowledge of their fields, confidently defined issues and crises in ways that only their colleagues or peers could fully understand. Since lay persons could not always know whether the "professional" was talking sense or nonsense, they frequently felt compelled to accept the diagnosis and prescription of the professional on faith. Since professionals routinely justified their actions by appealing to scientific fact, it became a major function of the university "to render universal scientific standards credible to the public."[15]

Seventeenth-century science became the new authority in American society. Rather than tackling issues or problems head-on, Americans learned to let the university-trained expert do it. Americans became passive, even submissive, since it was assumed that most if not all problems could best be solved by the expert, employing the techniques and knowledge of science. As Bledstein explains, science, as cultivated by the university

> implied more than method and procedure...It revealed hard, documentable realities within the fluid American environment; it bolstered the self-certainty of the specialist which only the foolhardy would dare contest; it separated the professional expert who defined the limits of the possible in a given social instance from the amateur reformer who wished to make the entire world over by moralizing every issue.[16]

In all fairness it must be said that substantial progress has been achieved by experts applying scientific principles to a multitude of social problems. In many ways the American faith in professionalization has been justified. Still, there are difficulties with this Cartesian legacy. Perhaps we have carried a good thing too far. The emphasis in the twentieth century on greater and greater specialization has, suggests Wilshire, eroded "the public service aspect of professionalism." Wilshire adds that "as professionals become engulfed in ever more specialized groups, and more and more groups contribute to any given outcome, each specialist's feeling of responsibility for the whole is diminished."[17] In an attempt to illustrate this tendency of professionalism to abandon its public role, discussions of the professionalization of the fields of philosophy and educational philosophy follow.

THE PROFESSIONALIZATION OF PHILOSOPHY

The modern university is often referred to as a "knowledge" factory where discoveries are made and assertions or beliefs produced that can be, in some sense, verified. Such an institution has advanced knowledge, particularly if we view knowledge as an aggregate of the specialized labors investigating particular fields or subfields in isolation, but it is not an educational institution. Education involves making sense of things, and that, notes Wilshire, "is an organismic activity."[18] As the modern American university evolved out of the "old time college," disciplined based departments, connected to national professional organizations, emerged as the dominant organizational structure for American higher education. With faculty loyalties within such departments increasingly drawn toward specializing the field and toward the national professional organization, support for the university's "sense making" role declined. A definitive answer to why this occurred is not possible, but the movement toward professionalism had become so much a part of the American experience that even academics involved in the rise of the university failed to critically examine its assumptions or think through its implication.

It is particularly ironic that philosophers, the group supposedly skilled in fleshing out underlying assumptions and probable implications, were also swept up in this movement toward professionalization. As Wilshire explains, "What Descartes had begun...could not really be stopped or even controlled. ...His notion of pure reason, technical and mathematical, is a revolutionary departure, and paves the way for the masking of the background and for secularizing and "scientizing" thought of all kinds."[19] One kind of thought offers us the ultimate test. If philosophy, the field that traditionally knew no boundaries, could be professionalized, then it could happen to any field.

As explained in an earlier chapter, the capstone course in moral philosophy dominated the curriculum of the "old time college," but in the modern university the natural sciences are generally regarded as the most important field. Some questioned philosophy's ability to survive in the science-oriented modern American university. Given the changed circumstances described previously, many academic philosophers decided to switch rather than fight. These philosophers chose to emulate the sciences by professionalizing the discipline. This meant creating a national association and, in emulation of the natural sciences, identifying a single, correct method of inquiry. Establishing such an association proved to be relatively easy, but the search for such a method of inquiry became much more problematic.

Such a professional association was formed in 1901 as eleven philosophers met in New York City and established the American Philosophical Association. J. E. Creighton, of Cornell University, took the lead in creating such an institution and served as its first president. Aware of the progress made by the natural sciences in recent decades and alarmed at philosophy's failure to keep pace, Creighton and his associates sought a new method of inquiry to assist philosophy in recouping some of the ground that it had lost in recent years. The search for such a method lead to Socrates and his interest in clarifying fundamental terms. Though philosophers could and should be careful in using language to convey their intended meanings in their writings, Creighton suggested that complete clarity could be best achieved through Socratic dialogue each year at professional meetings among those sanctioned as professional philosophers. No matter how carefully and clearly philosophers express themselves in written form, the danger that another philosopher reading their work will not fully understand it or interpret it as intended is great. At a conference or national meeting the written word is "reinforced by the living personality"[20] of the philosopher and dialogue with others enables the author to clarify and explain any terms that may connote multiple meanings or are otherwise problematic. Through such a "Socratic" method, Creighton and his colleagues were optimistic that solutions to age-old philosophical problems could be attained. In this way, philosophy, in emulation of the natural sciences, could justify its existence as a specialized, professional field.

This need to compete with the natural sciences accounts for, in part, Creighton and his associates' selective interpretation of the "Socratic" method. As Janice Moulton suggests, those seeking to professionalize the field of philosophy embraced the "Socratic method" as a "model of adversarial reasoning,"[21] that is, a duel or debate between adversaries. From Moulton's perspective, Creighton and others misinterpreted 'elenchus' to mean a method of discussion that aimed at demonstrating the error or wrongheadedness of the other or others' point of view. A more correct view of the term, suggests Moulton, is to think of it as a method of discussion that aims not to refute or rebut, but to challenge one's most cherished convictions. This latter approach enables those participating in the dialogue to engage in philosophical inquiry with a more open mind.

Those seeking to professionalize philosophy rejected this natural link to education, embracing instead the adversarial form of the "Socratic method." More often than not, this method was employed in a competitive effort "to win a point rather than convince."[22] For Creighton and others, this form of adversarial reasoning became the one correct method of *doing* philosophy. From this perspective, the intimate connection between philosophy and education is denied for Socrates is portrayed as an "ironic and insincere debater" rather than as "a playful and helpful teacher."[23] This "Socratic method" is but a means of enhancing one's own personal and professional prestige by overwhelming an opponent with one's wit and argumentative prowess. Rather than a method for encouraging others to think for themselves, this adversarial form of reasoning separated philosophy from its pedagogical roots. It is not surprising that Professor Creighton clearly articulated this perspective in his inaugural address as the first president of the American Philosophical Association, stating that "it would be a mistake to make the discussion of methods of teaching philosophy a coordinate purpose, even to introduce papers on this subject into the program of meetings."[24] Creighton did not want this new professional association to be composed of mere teachers of philosophy, but thought it should be an association for those professionals engaged in *doing* philosophy, that is, those who engage in the adversarial form of the "Socratic method." Wilshire suggests that "this foretells the course of professional philosophy in this century."[25]

In seeking to become professionalized, philosophy abandoned its pedagogical roots. Philosophers rejected the more traditional idea that their role was to foster cooperative effort between the young and old, to assist each of us in making sense of the world, and to instruct individuals and societies to live sanely. Such a task cannot be the domain of any specialized, professional field. All of us must assume responsibility for this task, for, in a philosophical and educational sense, we are all *amateurs*, pursuing wisdom and meaning for the love of it.

Though the American Philosophical Association experienced rapid growth during its formative years, not everyone agreed that the perennial problems of philosophy would succumb to the correct method of inquiry. Notably, William James initially rejected an invitation to join the association (James subsequently joined and served as president) noting that "philosophy discussion proper only succeeds between intimates who have learned how to converse by months of weary trial and failure. The philosopher is a lone beast dwelling in his individual burrow. Count me out!"[26] This is a remarkable statement. James suggests that essential differences exist between science and philosophy and that philosophy is best done among friends. It takes time for genuine philosophical dialogue to develop. To participate in such an activity means subordinating one's own ego in order to create a sense of trust among all participants so that everyone can contribute to this never-ending quest for meaning. From this perspective, philosophy remains much more complex and mysterious than Creighton's and others conceptualization of it. From this perspective, the belief that through an analytic process, congruent and allied with science, philosophers could discover the structure of the universe, was a bogus one. In embracing the Cartesian legacy and joining hands with the scientists "in a joint secular effort to break down the universe into its ultimate individual components, and reassemble the aggregate through calculation,"[27] academic philosophy, suggest James and others, was headed in the wrong direction.

This drive toward professionalization triumphed during the first three-quarters of the twentieth century. As Wilshire explains, "so caught up in one form or another of logical expertise were most philosophers that all sense of history was lost,.."[28] The result was the breaking up of philosophy into clearly defined subspecialties with clearly delineated standards to measure accomplishments in each. What began in 1902 as an intimate association between fifteen colleagues has evolved into an 8,000 member professional organization where hundreds of papers are presented at the national meeting each year. Creighton's and others' efforts to professionalize philosophy succeeded beyond their wildest dreams. What was intended to be a collegial, albeit tough-minded discussion among a relatively small group of "professional" philosophers has evolved into a cold, lifeless mechanical process that is more concerned with advancing the prestige and credentials of participants and the profession than with fostering greater understanding of truth and meaning. Perhaps Creighton and others interested in professionalizing the field did not intend this, but the consequence of such professionalization is philosophers confronting one another more like lawyers in a courtroom than as intimates trying to expand understanding in a common quest for meaning.

Before concluding this section on the APA's role in the professionalization of the field, it should be noted that voices clamoring for a more pluralistic vision of philosophy are being heard. Change is in the wind, but before discussing these changes and possible directions for the future, let us turn now to a discussion of the professionalization of one so-called subspecialty of philosophy—educational philosophy and the role that the Philosophy of Education Society and the John Dewey Society played in this process.

PROFESSIONALIZING EDUCATIONAL PHILOSOPHY

James Kaminsky suggests that "Philosophy of Education began at the Hotel Traymore, Atlantic City, on Sunday, 24th, February, 1935"[29] with the establishment of the John Dewey Society for the Study of Education and Culture. This new society was created by a group of educators concerned over our world's current economic and social crises and who believed that education could play a stronger role in restructuring the American democratic order. To their credit these educators, including philosophers, other academics, and schoolmen, "realized that the deepest and widest philosophical questions relating to the democratic prospect were not in the province of philosophers talking among themselves, but vital concerns of school people and the public at large."[30]

Announcing the new organization in its February, 1936 issue, *The Social Frontier* explained that:

> The new society was named for John Dewey, not because its founders wished to devote themselves to an exposition of the teachings of America's greatest educator and thinker, but rather because they felt in his life and work he represents the soundest and most hopeful approach to the study of the problems of education. For more than a generation he has proclaimed the social nature of the educative process and emphasized the close interdependence of school and society. Presumably, without being bound by his philosophy, the John Dewey Society will work out of the tradition which John Dewey has done more than any other person to create...[31]

Whether the Society has succeeded in this attempt to emulate, rather than mimic, John Dewey's approach remains problematic, but it is clear that the founders did not think of this new society as just another professional association designed to promote a particular field. To suggest, as Kaminsky does, that the discipline of educational philosophy began with the establishment of "a "learned guild' for the purpose of supplying a specific research program consistent with the intellectual ambitions of said "learned guild,'"[32] denies the intimate relationship between philosophy and education that Dewey champions.

Throughout its history, the John Dewey Society has survived, if not flourished, by vacillating between social activism promoting education's role in restructuring democracy and mimicking other professional associations promoting academic fields. The organization that once sponsored *The Social Frontier* and its proactive treatment of the major social and educational issues of the day has evolved into a typical professional association that, along with the Philosophy of Education Society, sponsors *Educational Theory*, the professional journal for educational theorists and philosophers.

The John Dewey Society has retained one distinguishing characteristic from its formative years. Today, as in the past, membership in the Society is not limited to those whose professional interests are directed at educational philosophy and theory. Still, the organization is dominated by members affiliated with university schools or colleges of education. Given the emphasis that universities place upon traditional research, the decision, after more than a quarter of a century of presenting the annual Dewey lecture at the American Association of Colleges of Teacher Education meeting in Chicago, to present the lecture each year at the annual meeting of the American Educational Research Association is not surprising. Both associations are dominated by academics but, since it is in teacher education where the theorist and practitioner meet, it seems symbolically more appropriate for a lecture sponsored by the society and named after John Dewey to be associated with the AACTE. While the Society has struggled to keep Dewey's vision of the intimate connection between philosophy and education in focus, it has evolved into just another professional association, supporting another academic, albeit somewhat broader, field or approach.

If, as suggested above, the John Dewey Society reluctantly succumbed to the pressures of professionalization, the Philosophy of Education Society willingly embraced professionalization as the vehicle that could bring this emerging field academic respectability. Educational philosophy continues to suffer from an inferiority complex. Always desiring but never fully gaining the respect of "real" academic philosophers, educational philosophers followed, four decades later, the lead of the parent discipline, creating a professional association to promote educational philosophy as an academic discipline. R. Bruce Raup of Teachers College, Columbia took the lead, circulating in November of 1940 a letter to colleagues around the country suggesting that they form a national association to promote the teaching and study of philosophy of education.[33] A planning meeting followed on February 22, 1941 at the Hotel Adelphia in Philadelphia resulting in the formation of the Philosophy of Education Society.

Raup and others sought to distinguish between those engaged in the "discipline of philosophizing" from the mere amateur in the field. A part of the first meeting was devoted to establishing the criteria for distinguishing between "fellows" and associates of the society. Acceptance as a "fellow" in the society was to be determined by one's commitment to and accomplishments in the field. The intent here is to control what counts as educational philosophy and who is admitted to the guild.

As Giarelli and Chambliss explain, the language used by Raup and others was one of "exclusion, distinctiveness, economic interest, and selective initiation."[34] In his letter proposing the formation of such a society, Raup identifies the purposes that the association would serve. It is interesting that extending and improving the teaching of educational philosophy was not among his top three priorities. It is not surprising that "the promotion of the fundamental philosophical treatment of the problems of education..."[35] was Raup's primary purpose, but it is telling that he considered both cultivating the relationship with general philosophy and recruiting promising students into the field to be more important goals than improving the teaching of educational philosophy. In the constitution of the Philosophy of Education Society adopted in 1958, teaching is more prominently mentioned, but, like the APA, it has never been a primary concern of the Philosophy of Education Society.

With the founding of the Philosophy of Education Society, educational philosophy embraced professionalism. Doing so meant an educational philosopher must demonstrate command of the distinctive subject matter and methodology that supposedly defines the field. The question remained whether any such essential subject matter or unique methodology exists. Some, including John Childs, claimed that "modern philosophy has largely abandoned the earlier pretense that it had privileged access to the ultimate nature of reality and to the final meaning and good of life."[36] Such a claim posed a problem for the Philosophy of Education Society and for those advocating the professionalization of the field.

What is educational philosophy's distinctive function and upon what metaphysical foundation is the authority of educational philosophy built? Throughout this century educational philosophers, embracing professionalism, have attempted to justify their distinct or special status by appealing to either the "isms or system-building" approach or to the "analytic" approach as the one, correct metaphysical or methodological foundation. Under the rubric of philosophy *of* and philosophy *and* education, these approaches are discussed in detail in an earlier chapter. They are reintroduced here to point out that either or both have been used in support of educational philosophy's claim "to professional distinctiveness and legitimacy...."[37]

During the 1950s and 1960s, this desire for academic credibility became an obsession to some. The apparent need for some members of PES to repeatedly demonstrate to the "pure" philosophers that educational philosophers could do "pure" philosophy made for some peculiar sessions at the annual PES meetings. Such a state of affairs caused one prominent member to wonder in 1958 "just how much *education* do we concern ourselves with?" Reporting as one who had attended all of the annual meetings of the Philosophy of Education Society, Ernest Bayles recalled "few programs dealing directly and forthrightly with problems of education."[38]

Though there is little documentation of the first decade and a half of the society's existence, Bayles's assessment of the society was shared by other prominent members of the society such as Harry S. Broudy and Kenneth D. Benne. If discussions of educational problems were given short shrift during the early years of the society, little, if any, improvement was achieved during the 1960s and 1970s. During this period analytic philosophy rose to prominence in the Philosophy of Education Society, further segregating educational philosophers from the problems of school practice. As educational philosophers seemed bent on making "ever-finer conceptual distinctions,"[39] some members of the society wondered if members were talking only to themselves.

Jonas Soltis shared these concerns, admitting in 1975 that the educational philosopher was experiencing a bit of an identity crisis. Noting in his 1975 presidential address that educational philosophers had "sought responsibility and respectability by fuller immersion in and merger with general academic philosophy,"[40] Soltis recognized that educational philosophy could not be just another subfield of philosophy in general. Soltis suggested that the educational philosopher should not be compared to either the philosopher of history or the philosopher of science. While the philosopher of science or history may never feel compelled to do science or history, the educational philosopher feels the need to make a difference in both philosophy and education. Though Soltis admits that educational philosophers "feel guilty" for being identified as philosophers of education, he suggests that "we want to have some effect on the field of education and these are noble and proper feelings."[41]

Many educational philosophers appreciated the ambivalence that Soltis identified in his presidential address, but little changed over the next few years. Subsequent meetings of the society found no more papers or sessions directly responding to issues of educational practice. The discourse may have been more analytic during this so-called middle period of PES (Tozer divides the history of the Philosophy of Education Society into three periods beginning in 1941), but, like the earlier period, discussion of educational practice rarely entered the society's mainstream.

More attention has been devoted to educational issues in recent meetings of PES, but Tozer characterizes this as unusual and cautions against thinking of this as a strong trend. Tozer suggests that the scarcity of PES papers on school reform and other educational issues is attributable, in part, to educational philosophers' desire to use the PES annual meeting as the one place where they can engage in "pure" philosophizing. Tozer suggests that members of the society often belong to other professional education associations and frequently present at their annual meetings on more practical educational issues. This tendency of PES members to segregate their philosophizing from their other roles as members of the education professorate is illustrative of the "sense of guilt" that many educational philosophers feel.

This sense of inferiority is based on the questionable assumption that the philosophy of education is just another subfield of philosophy proper. Isn't it time for educational philosophers to outgrow this sense of guilt? Educational philosophy impacts (or should impact) education as well as philosophy. For this reason, it seems reasonable to expect the national association most closely connected to the field to equally balance or integrate presentations on philosophy and education at its annual meetings.

Voices raised in support of the society becoming a more pluralistic forum, to repeat Bayles's plea, for dealing "directly and forthrightly with problems of education" are being heard, but, to some, the Philosophy of Education Society remains an exclusive, and somewhat arrogant group. This perception is captured best in the response of a qualified minority when asked why he did not attend PES meetings. After suggesting that the adversarial style that characterizes many PES sessions discourages one "trying something a little bit different,"[42] the respondent added that the Philosophy of Education Society is a bit like a private club. Unless you know everybody, you feel like an intruder. In its attempt to raise educational philosophy to equal status with real or "pure" philosophy, the Philosophy of Education Society developed into an association promoting distinctiveness and authority. In doing so, it has become an almost textbook example of a national association advocating the professionalization of a field.

THE WINDS OF CHANGE

Both the Philosophy of Education Society and the American Philosophical Association remain committed to the culture of professionalism. Movements within each organization supporting a more pluralistic view of philosophy have achieved some minor successes, but neither association has embraced teaching as its primary goal. In this regard, they lag behind other professional associations that have recently emphasized the improvement of teaching as a means of promoting better understanding of a field and its relationship to other fields. For example, The Modern Language Association has organized, as part of its annual meetings, institutes on teaching. The American Mathematical Association initiated a nationwide investigation into the reasons why so many students fail college calculus courses. This resulted in a review and revision of the curriculum and a more careful consideration of teaching techniques. The point here is that professional associations have a role to play in promoting good teaching in the field they represent.[43] One wonders why the APA or especially the Philosophy of Education Society have not taken the lead in improving the quality of teaching. It is ironic that the associations affiliated with the academic fields most concerned with developing an understanding of truth or meaning have lagged behind other associations in emphasizing teaching.

For the APA and PES to rediscover the connection between philosophy and pedagogy would be a step in the right direction. However, it is not a panacea for the problems associated with professionalism. The complementary relationship between professionalism and the emergence of the modern university resulted in a narrow definition of what counts as scholarship. In order to remedy the abuses of overspecialization that accompanied the drive toward professionalization, we must, Boyer suggests, reconsider the priorities of the professoriate. In addition to valuing and rewarding traditional scholarship, "It is time," says Donald Kennedy, former President of Stanford University, "for us to reaffirm that education—that is, teaching in all its forms—is the primary task" of higher education.[44] President Kennedy's remarks offer a ray of hope, but currently only research that purports to discover principles or truths that define increasingly narrow fields or subfields counts as legitimate scholarship at the university.

In keeping with Kennedy's admonition and to balance an overemphasis on traditional research, Boyer recommends that universities recognize the scholarship of integration, application, and teaching as equal to that of discovery or traditional research. These domains of scholarship overlap, but the scholarship of integration, application, and teaching addresses the educational mission of institutions of higher education. Of particular interest to philosophers is the scholarship of integration. For the university to perform its educative role, it is crucial for professors to assist students in making connections across the disciplines, to help them place their specialties in larger contexts, and to help students and colleagues in examining data or "facts" from different perspectives. To engage in this kind of scholarship is a rigorous intellectual activity, involving familiarity with "overlapping {academic} neighborhoods."[45] Since historically, philosophy has been concerned with all fields of knowledge, philosophers are ideally suited to engage in this kind of scholarly activity. Such scholarship serves a very useful purpose for it enables both the student and the expert to fit research findings into larger intellectual patterns. In this way such scholarship enables those aspiring to be professionals and the experts themselves to avoid the pitfalls associated with over-specialization.

If philosophers in general are well suited to focus on the scholarship of integration, educational philosophers seem well suited to concentrate on the scholarship of application. As Boyer describes this kind of scholarship, the key questions are "How can knowledge be responsibly applied to consequential problems? How can it be helpful to individuals as well as institutions? Can social problems *themselves* define an agenda for scholarly investigation?"[46] These first two questions bring to mind Bayles's comment regarding the lack of PES sessions "dealing directly and forthrightly with problems of education." The third question echoes a comment made by Stephen Tozer in his article "PES and School Reform." In discussing whether problems of school reform are sufficiently philosophical to merit the attention of members of the society, Tozer suggests that educational philosophers have not looked hard enough for the intellectually demanding philosophical problems awaiting our discovery.

Here again lies the Cartesian legacy. Assuming that knowledge is first discovered and then applied, the scholarship of application is deemed worthy of only second-class minds. Contrary to this widely held view, the scholarship of application is a dynamic process with theory and practice interacting with and renewing one another. As Boyer suggests, "new intellectual understandings can arise out of the very act of application."[47] While the focus may be on application, the activities of discovery and application occur virtually simultaneously.

The scholarship of application is the step-child of American higher education. Usually associated with professional schools or professional programs, this kind of scholarship is often derided for not being academic or intellectually rigorous enough. Accepting that their mission is somehow inferior, these professional schools and programs seek academic respectability by mimicking the arts and sciences. Though their explicit purpose is to connect theory and practice, such schools or programs tend to emphasize theory at the expense of practice. In order to compete in a university organized in accordance with Cartesian principles, professional schools emphasize "a more academic and less practical view of what their students need to know."[48]

While philosophy proper and educational philosophy are well suited for the scholarship of integration and application respectively, the scholarship of teaching is natural to both fields. Unfortunately, teaching is usually not thought of as a scholarly activity. Despite Aristotle's characterization of it as "the highest form of understanding," teaching takes a backseat to the more traditional research agenda of the modern university. Teaching that is done well, that is, teaching that involves transforming and extending as well as transmitting knowledge, is scholarship of the highest order. The failure of the modern university to recognize and reward such scholarship stems, in part, from the Cartesian dualism which suggests that knowledge or truth is a finite entity that, once mastered, can be passed on relatively easily from one to another. The dynamic nature of the teaching and learning process is demeaned as teaching becomes little more than passing on the predetermined truths to the uninitiated.

While research universities claim to value creative and scholarly teaching, their actions contradict their claims. Such institutions train the faculty for most American colleges and universities, but mastery of subject matter, not teaching, is emphasized. In most cases, doctoral students pursue a course of study aimed at preparing them for traditional research in their chosen specialty or for teaching a small number of highly motivated and knowledgeable graduate students. Instead, most faculty spend a good portion of their careers teaching large numbers of undergraduates who need help in placing specialized knowledge into a larger pattern or context and who require assistance in understanding how to apply specialized data in meaningful ways. As Boyer notes, "helping new professors prepare for this special work is an obligation graduate schools have, all too often, overlooked."[49]

To meet this obligation, Boyer suggests that teacher training become a part of every graduate program. He calls for a seminar on teaching to be team-taught by a professor in the appropriate specialty and by an education professor or someone knowledgeable of how students learn. The intent of the seminar would be to improve the pedagogical skills of doctoral students, but it should also enhance their understanding of the field itself. By recognizing that teaching a subject requires a deeper level of understanding, the graduate student begins to appreciate the scholarly value of teaching. What Boyer recommends for all graduate programs is crucial for the fields of education (including educational philosophy) because future professors of education need to model correct pedagogical practice for their students.

Boyer's call for such a seminar with graduate credit is long overdue. The time has come for philosophy in general and educational philosophy in particular to respond to these calls for radical change. There is some reason for optimism when prominent educational philosophers as Jonas Soltis propose that "study, training, and gaining familiarity with some mode of specialized educational practice like the teaching of a subject or of a grade level"[50] become required components in educational philosophy doctoral programs.

Establishing such programs that focus in significant ways on educational practice is a step in the right direction, but I wonder if Soltis's proposal goes far enough. His emphasis seems to be on the *study* of educational practice rather than on actually integrating, applying, or engaging educational practice in a direct and forthright manner. His ideal curriculum for preparing educational philosophers retains as its goal the preparation of professional educational philosophers who still possess specialized knowledge and skills. Clearly such attention to educational practice is needed, but Soltis's professional educational philosopher basks in the light at or near the entrance to the cave. Such a philosopher may consent to descending into the cave to show the practitioner the way, but such a descent is a matter of obligation rather than the philosopher's reason to be. For educational philosophers, if not all philosophers, their reason to be is informing educational practice.

THE ULTIMATE IRONY: PROMOTING THE PROFESSION OF TEACHING

It is ironic that educational philosophers must reorient themselves more toward the schools than the university if they are to satisfy their reason to be. Just as the schools or colleges of education need to make "the profession of education as their main point of reference," educational philosophers need to make educational practice their primary focus. As Clifford and Guthrie explain, it is not enough for schools of education to consider themselves as places where fundamental educational issues are studied "from a variety of disciplinary perspectives."[51] The field of educational philosophy has prided itself as being one of the most distinctive of the perspectives investigating educational issues, but, in assuming this elitist role, educational philosophers have contributed to the failure by schools and colleges of education to promote teaching as an honorable profession.

The school or college of education cannot abandon the scholarly inquiry into education in its many manifestations, but that scholarship must emphasize the integration, application, and teaching, as well as the discovery of knowledge. Educational philosophers should refrain from mimicking their counterparts in the university's philosophy departments. As Clifford and Guthrie note, it is difficult to "best the disciplinary departments at their own game,"[52] but, more importantly, their game conflicts with the goal that educational philosophers should embrace—namely, improving educational practice at all levels and in all places.

Educational philosophers and the field of educational philosophy has suffered for failing to embrace this role. By considering themselves engaged in the premier educational discipline, educational philosophers stand above and apart from others investigating educational practice. In attempting to become as academic as possible, educational philosophers alienated their natural colleagues and never gained full acceptance by academic or "real" philosophers. In hitching their wagon to the academic, professionalized vision of philosophy, educational philosophers not only denied their reason to be, but ensured for themselves a lonely, inconsequential professional or academic life.

The time has come for the field of educational philosophy to accept its mission as promoting the improvement of educational practice in all fields and at all levels. Such recognition means less emphasis on the distinctive nature of educational philosophy and closer collaboration with our colleagues in other educational foundation fields and in curriculum and methods. Such collaboration does not mean the abandonment of the philosophical and historical issues of education, but it does mean making a concerted effort to connect such issues "to what is so eminently observable in *any* school." To illustrate how this can be done, Richard Wisniewski points to Ron Podeschi's introductory foundations course at the University of Wisconsin-Milwaukee. In teaching the class in the real world setting of an urban school, Podeschi helps the students to understand the historical, philosophical, and sociological contexts for the realities they experience in this setting.[53]

Collaboration and collegiality is the key as educational philosophers must learn to communicate with educators at every level if the field or discipline is to play a role in improving the quality of education in our nation. Even those educational philosophers choosing to pursue a more traditional scholarly agenda need to realize that the time for distinctiveness has passed. A vision of educational philosophy as a distinctive, authoritarian, and professionalized field is no longer acceptable. Instead of thinking of educational philosophy as the foundation upon which all other studies of education are to be built, it is time to jettison the foundations metaphor. In its place Lee Shulman suggests that we think of educational philosophy and related fields "as scaffoldings, as the framework for pedagogy."[54] Rather than struggling to distinguish itself as a distinct discipline, educational philosophy could better serve its reason to be by reconstructing itself as a mode of inquiry that is integral to the structure of education itself. Embracing the scaffolding metaphor means losing the distinctive nature of educational philosophy, but such imagery reorients educational philosophy to its Deweyian roots. Reviving Dewey's vision of philosophy as education is the theme of a later chapter. For now it is enough to suggest that the ultimate irony is for educational philosophy to fulfill its reason to be, that is, to contribute to the development of teaching as an honorable profession, it must abandon its efforts to become a distinctive and professionalized academic discipline.

Postmodernist Critiques of Philosophy and Educational Philosophy

As noted in an earlier chapter, twentieth-century philosophy has been described as a revolt against classical rationalism. Such a description is appropriate for the first two-thirds of this century, but, more recently, the revolt has been extended to rationality itself. As Beyer and Liston suggest "'reason' itself is (being) subjected to a similar critique and dismissal."[1] The intent is not, suggests Foucault, to eliminate rationality but to prevent such questions as "*What* is this Reason that we use? What are its historical effects? What are its limits, and what are its dangers?"[2] from being ignored. This more recent postmodernism movement has been described as a "rage against reason," a revolt against the excesses and arrogance often associated with the twentieth-century manifestations of Enlightenment thought. These manifestations culminated in the specialization and fragmentation of knowledge and in the professionalization of the disciplines (see chapter 4). Even philosophy, the most encyclopedic of all fields of knowledge, succumbed to the siren song of professionalism, casting aside the well-read amateur in favor of the professionally trained philosopher. By mimicking science, particularly a seventeenth century view of science, twentieth-century philosophers embraced linguistic and logical analysis as *the* methodology capable of fulfilling their elusive quest for certainty. Midcentury British and American philosophers were especially confident that the means of discovering the truth, if not the truth itself, was now available to them.

As Russell Jacoby and others have noted, the generation of intellectuals initiated into full-blown academic professions, including philosophy and educational philosophy, during the post-World War II era, encountered "an enthusiastically developing or confidently stable paradigm of research that promised definitive answers to important problems."[3] This paradigm, often identified as structuralism, sought "rationality, linearity, progress, and control by discovering, developing, and inventing metanarratives, metadiscourses, and metacritiques that define rationality, linearity, progress and control."[4] The reasoning is circular in that it presupposes the existence of universal, transcendent, and foundational first principles or truths.

Discussions of such a foundation in its multiple forms are known as metanarratives, metadiscourses, or metacritiques. Philosophy has historically been associated with such metacritiques as virtually every philosopher since Socrates engaged in a search for certainty. From Plato to the present, philosophers have sought the ultimate foundation upon which to structure human civilization. During the Enlightenment, faith in the perfectibility of the human species through "reason" assumed metaphysical proportions. This belief in human reason as the penultimate vehicle for moving civilization forward reached its pinnacle in recent times as epistemology replaced metaphysics as the premier area of interest for philosophers.

From this perspective, knowing the means of attaining the truth replaced knowing the truth as the definitive characteristic of philosophy. Even if philosophers of the modern world were unwilling to assert that they knew the truth, their use of linguistic and logical analysis to assess the validity of competing knowledge claims reestablished philosophy's position as a, if not the, foundational discipline. From this perspective, philosophy supposedly offered insights into or access to the principles upon which all other structures are based. Grounded in religious, metaphysical, or epistemological first principles, metanarratives promised "order, organization, and certainty." When applied to education, such metanarratives implied "accountability, efficiency, and control."[5]

But what if there are no transcendent first principles? Doubting the existence of these first principles assumed almost faddish proportions in recent decades. Continental philosophers such as Foucault and Derrida fleshed out the darker side of this Enlightenment faith in reason. Demonstrating that the Enlightenment's commitment to "communicative rationality *can* potentially" become "suffocating straitjackets" and "enslaving conceptions,"[6] Derrida points out that the "conversation of mankind" touted by Rorty and others is just that "—a conversation of *mankind*, primarily white mankind."[7] Derrida, by forcing us to see that our cherished 'age of reason' was to some, "whether they be women,

Blacks, or others bludgeoned by exclusionary tactics," less than enlightened, chipped away at the foundational armor of reason itself. Derrida brings into question the efficacy of dialogue as a means of solving human problems by "teaching us how much can go wrong,—even tragically wrong—in the folds of communication."[8]

As Lyotard suggests, it is this "distrust of Metanarratives" that defines the postmodernist attitude. Taking this a step further, Cherryholmes explains that "postmodern, post analytic, and post structural thought are skeptical and incredulous about the possibility of such metanarratives."[9] If all metanarratives are, at best, illusory foundations, the question becomes upon what basis can any commitment to any belief or course of action be grounded?

Is there no way around the "grand Either/Or (as Bernstein calls it): *either* there is a rational grounding of the norms of critique *or* the conviction that there is such a rational grounding is itself a self-deceptive illusion."[10] It has been suggested that the postmodern movement offers new genres of critique that escape the Scylla of groundless critique on the one hand, and the Charybdis of a rationally grounded critique that is illusory on the other hand.[11]

Is this so? Once the postmodernists lay bare the false presuppositions upon which modern societies are based, what is offered as an alternative? After effectively debunking the modern world and its institutions, do postmodernists have the energy and vision to reconstruct that which they demean and despise? In educational terms, if there are no essential or canonical truths, what should be taught? Is there any meaningful difference between indoctrination and education? Are we left impotent by the postmodernist critiques unable or unwilling to remake the world in accordance with a justifiable moral vision? Are we afloat in a dead calm sea concerned only with maintaining the status quo?

It has been suggested that postmodernists are travelling along a path previously traversed by John Dewey, but it remains to be seen whether these postmodernist critiques lead to a revival of the critical pragmatism of Dewey or serve as an apology for contemporary bourgeois liberalism. These larger questions are fleshed out in this and the following chapter.

If philosophy, in its current postmodernist manifestation, is following along a path blazed by Dewey and other pragmatists, what is that path like? A parable by Franz Kafka offers insights into the philosophical journey. In the parable a traveler encounters two antagonists. One blocks the road ahead while the other presses him from behind. As Richard J. Bernstein explains, the philosopher, that is, the traveler, is caught in the middle between the warring forces of the past and future.

Perhaps it is natural for the philosopher to desire to "jump out of the firing line" and assume the role of a neutral umpire, but it is not possible.[12] Many have tried but the possibility of attaining what Rorty calls a "god's eye view" is an illusion. The philosopher's place is in this gap between the past and the future. The conflict is never over and there is never a definitive winner or loser. If the philosopher succumbs to either of these binary opposites, thinking stops and the philosophic pilgrimage is over. If the philosopher joins forces with the past, she becomes little more than a disciple of some tradition and ceases to think for herself. If all energies and abilities are expended in destroying the past, then the philosopher surrenders herself to an unknown future, trusting that any future must be better than the devil that she knows and destroyed.

Given the nature of this dilemma, it is not surprising that philosophers have spent much of their collective history in a search for certainty, that is, seeking a methodological or metaphysical platform from which to observe and direct the final outcome. The recent postmodernist critique has effectively illuminated the failure of such attempts, but one also wonders whether in doing so if the postmodernists gore themselves on the other horn of this dilemma. In deconstructing the "past," postmodernist critiques have performed a very useful and necessary function. Still their critique falls short by failing to articulate a vision of a plausible and desirable future. In addition to pushing back the past, a philosopher must at times use the past to confront the prejudices of the present and their possible future manifestations. Postmodernist philosophers expended their energy destroying the "past," but offer few ideas and little intellectual energy for reconstructing the future. In this sense, they too have succumbed to what Dewey calls either/or thinking.

WHY RORTY?

In an attempt to understand and assess the impact that postmodernism themes are having on philosophy and educational philosophy, Richard Rorty's work is discussed here in some depth. A discussion of his works seems particularly relevant since his "provocative interpretations of the present impasse in analytic philosophy impel philosophers to examine the problematic status of their subject."[13] With the publication of his *Philosophy and the Mirror of Nature* (1979), Rorty did for philosophy in general what Thomas Kuhn's *The Structure of Scientific Revolutions* did for the philosophy of science. This work by Rorty has been described as the most important work in American philosophy since Dewey's *The Quest for Certainty*, in part, because he "creatively appropriated 'postmodern' themes."[14]

For the first time, an insider, a well-respected member of the Anglo-American community of analytic philosophers, had embraced themes typically associated with Continental philosophy. His analysis, in suggesting "that modern North Atlantic philosophy has... come to an end"[15] was all the more shocking since analytic philosophers historically had ignored Continental philosophy, considering it to be "a quagmire of confusion, obfuscation, and pretentious gesturing—flouting even the most minimal standard of clarity and rational argumentation."[16]

With the publication of Rorty's seminal work in 1979, postmodernist themes entered the philosophical mainstream and forced professional philosophers to critically examine their own field. Our purpose in reviewing Rorty's work is to understand the nature of the postmodernist critique and to assess its impact on both philosophy and educational philosophy. Of particular concern is the role that the postmodernists' critiques are having in redefining educational philosophy's reason to be. More specifically, the question is to what extent postmodernism assists us in understanding the role of philosopher as pilgrim. With these concerns in mind, we turn now to Rorty's work, offering first an overview of his thought followed by more critical assessment of his educational ideas and views on the relationship of philosophy to democracy. Our discussion of Rorty concludes with a discussion of the efficacy of Rorty's thought and that of other postmodernists in fostering and sustaining moral action.

RORTY: AN OVERVIEW

Philosophy and the Mirror of Nature represents a substantive departure from Rorty's earlier work, but equally striking is his style which is dramatically different from that usually associated with analytic philosophers. As Cornel West explains, Rorty's style "rests upon scholarly erudition and literary flair," and "ingeniously combines critical expository analysis and illuminating historical narrative." In further describing the style that was to become Rorty's trademark, West suggests that Rorty moves from "technical argumentation to cultural commentary with ease and wit."[17] Despite the complexities of the material he is discussing, Rorty's works are remarkably free of technical and academic jargon. For this reason his works are more interesting than most philosophical texts and accessible to the educated amateur as well as to the professional philosopher. In this sense, Rorty practices what he preaches.

Rorty's opposition to modern philosophy's infatuation with science places him squarely within the postmodernist movement. He character-izes the question that modern philosophers ask: "How is it that science has had so much success?" as a bad question that produced an even worse answer. The answer that "the New Science discovered the language which nature itself uses"[18] caused philosophers to mimic scientists by searching for ever more definitive representations of the objective reality assumed to exist outside the mind. Ultimately such a search resulted in epistemology assuming an increasingly significant role in the field of phi-losophy. A theory that could explain how the mind constructs represen-tations of an objective, natural reality became the holy grail of modern philosophical thought. Assuming that such an objective, natural reality exists meant that the world could be ordered in accordance with the degree of accuracy with which various and competing theories of repre-sentation mirror nature.[19]

John Dewey, in *The Quest for Certainty*, suggests that this need for certainty characterizes the modern human condition. In a similar fashion, Rorty implies that a desire for constraint characterizes the dominant con-temporary human condition. In short, the modern world's infatuation with science has resulted in "the desire for a theory of knowledge (which) is a desire for constraint—a desire to find foundations to which one might cling, frameworks beyond which one could not stray, objects which impose themselves, representations which cannot be gainsaid."[20]

For both Dewey and Rorty, these desires are the product of cultures during a particular stage of their ongoing evolution, but modern-day philosophers erroneously assumed that these desires reflect a universal, natural human essence that is essentially rational. Based upon a complex set of assumptions, being fully human came to mean being rational. Being rational meant developing a theory of representation that would apply to all things. Constructing such a theory meant discovering the common ground that must exist among all things. "To suggest, as Rorty does, that there is *no* such common ground seems to endanger rationali-ty."[21] At the very least such a denial plays havoc with a philosophical tra-dition dominated by epistemology.

This quest for certainty, this desire for constraint, are part of a larg-er effort by modern human beings "to give sense to their lives"[22] by plac-ing them within a larger context. Humans have devised two traditional ways of doing this, suggests Rorty. The more common way involves humans describing "themselves as standing in immediate relation to a nonhuman reality." Rorty characterizes this more common approach as the "desire for objectivity."[23] Contemporary Western civilization has evolved from this more dominant tradition—" a tradition which runs from the Greek philosophers through the enlightenment"[24] and a tradition that is characterized by the search for the *Truth* for its own sake. In this tradition Kafka's traveler (our philosopher) struggles "to step outside (her) community long enough to examine it in the light of something which transcends it,..."[25] Rorty calls those who embrace this objectivist tradition *realists.*

Another method humans employ in making sense of their lives "is by telling the story of their contribution to a community. This community may be the actual historical one in which they live, or another actual one, distant in time or place, or a quite imaginary one, consisting perhaps of a dozen heroes or heroines."[26] Humans choosing this approach reduce the desire for objectivity to a desire for solidarity. They search, not for metaphysical or epistemological truth, but for "truths" that are good for humans to believe.[27] From this perspective, to declare a certain fact to be true is "simply a compliment paid to the beliefs which we think so well justified that, for the moment, further justification is not needed."[28]

For the *pragmatist,* as Rorty labels those who, like himself, seek solidarity, the goal is never to stand aside or above and judge how well the community measures up to some "ideal" standard, but to extend the community as far as possible. For the pragmatist, it is always possible that some new evidence may be forthcoming to either reinforce or debunk currently held beliefs. From this perspective, there is no a priori common ground. There is no final or ultimate truth upon which to validate human action, and there is no correct methodology that, when mastered, will enable humanity to answer all of life's mysteries. Still, all is not lost. Humankind has learned how to reason and that by reasoning together progress in resolving human dilemmas is possible.

Human progress is possible, not in the Enlightenment sense of rationally defining, systematically attacking, and scientifically solving complex puzzles, but by what Rorty calls muddling through—perhaps best illustrated by the haphazard and often nonrational means one uses to progress from adolescence to adulthood. Rorty suggests that even such a paradigm case of muddling through is not entirely arbitrary or capricious. Those involved in becoming an adult or in assisting in that process have an obligation to talk to one another, "to use persuasion rather than force, to be tolerant of diversity, to be contritely fallibist."[29] The obligation to behave in such a fashion is not derived from some transcendent first principle, but from practical advantages such behavior has produced in similar situations. Rorty suggests that this kind of muddling through is all that we can expect.

There are times when a particular society or culture may achieve—usually through coercion or compulsion—a great deal of consensus on what counts as evidence. It is during these times of what Kuhn calls normal science that epistemology dominates. Clearly the objectivist tradition described above has dominated the recent history of the modern world. In a sense, the pragmatists and the Continental philosophers have joined forces in attacking this "modern" tradition. By debunking this tradition and the philosophies upon which it is based, Rorty and others suggest that contemporary Western civilization is in an analogous position to scientists when the dominant paradigm of normal science has been debunked. Like the "new fuzzies" in the philosophy of science, all we can do is muddle through, "hoping that some reweaving will happen on both sides (competing paradigms) and that some consensus may thus emerge."[30] Rorty suggests that solidarity achieved by muddling through is the more desirable human condition since it is clear that the objectivist tradition is no longer, if it ever was, viable.

Much of Rorty's work described previously is reminiscent of, yet different from, Dewey's attempt in *Experience and Education* to identify and warn against falling prey to the either/or fallacy. If one's actions are no more than a reaction to that which is deemed wrong of another's position, little is accomplished. Put another way, it is not enough to tear down that which you do not like or with which you disagree. Unless one has a vision of what should be, destroying what is serves no useful purpose. Rorty and other postmodernists are very good at "deconstructing" the modern world, but is "muddling through" sufficient for reconstructing a more effective and humane society? In hopes of gaining insights into these and other questions, Rorty's educational ideas and his views on philosophy and democracy are discussed in the sections that follow.

RORTY'S EDUCATIONAL IDEAS: PHILOSOPHY AS EDIFICATION

In rejecting the notion "that man has an essence—namely to discover essences,"[31] a notion shared by Platonists, Kantians, and Positivists alike, Rorty has revived the position Dewey articulated fifty years earlier. Rather than conceiving of philosophy as foundational, we should, suggests Rorty, think of philosophy as a poetic, edifying enterprise "designed to make the reader question his own motives for philosophizing rather than to supply him with a new philosophical program."[32]

Rorty defines "edification" as the process "of finding new, better, more interesting, more fruitful ways of speaking."[33] It may involve making connections between our culture and some exotic culture or historical period, or between our own discipline and another discipline. Unlike more systematic philosophers who construct arguments designed to prove or persuade, edifying philosophers employ the tools of artists and offer satires, parodies, and aphorisms. Systematic philosophers write for eternity, constructing great mansions resting on metaphysical or scientific pillars. Edifying philosophers "destroy for the sake of their generation." Systematic philosophers are engaged in the quest for certainty, but edifying philosophers "want to keep space open for the sense of wonder which poets can sometimes cause—wonder that there is something new under the sun, something which is not an accurate representation of what was already there, something which (at least for the moment) cannot be explained and can barely be described."[34]

Rorty suggests that if we lose this sense of wonder, if we answer all questions definitively, then philosophy ends and some sort of science or theology begins. If systematic philosophers succeed in making a science of philosophy, then philosophy becomes just another boring academic subject. Perhaps this explains why educational philosophy, taught from either the "implicative" or "applicative" view, is such a boring and meaningless subject for many students.

Philosophy as a foundational discipline has become, suggests Rorty, an arrogant, pompous, and ignored discipline. If philosophy is to contribute to the creation of a better world, it must abandon its foundational claims to unique insights regarding truths or ways to the truth and accept a lesser, more humble, yet significant role. Instead of guiding all of humankind to the truth, philosophy must be content with "keeping a conversation going." Wisdom remains the philosophical goal, but for an edifying philosopher wisdom means understanding human beings "as generations of new descriptions rather than beings one hopes to be able to describe accurately."[35] If wisdom is equated with some objective truth, humans become objects rather than subjects. In short, a philosophy that aims at directing the individual toward some special objective truth does not treat that individual with respect.

As already noted, human beings need, in order to make sense of their lives, to place themselves within a larger context. Reminiscent of both Dewey and Jerome Bruner, Rorty suggests that there are two ways of doing this. We can try to determine what, if any, is our relationship to some nonhuman reality, or we can construct our own individual story of our contribution to a community. Referring to the former as the desire for objectivity, Rorty asserts that not only is such an approach disrespectful of humans, but it simply does not work anymore. The latter is the better choice for practical reasons. By choosing to construct our own story, we can "think of human progress as making it possible for human beings to do more interesting things, and be more interesting people...Our self-image would employ images of making rather than finding, the images used by the romantics to praise poets rather than the images used by the Greeks to praise mathematicians."[36]

In rejecting systematic foundational philosophy's perception of truth, goodness, and beauty as unproblematical, Rorty joins Dewey in suggesting that philosophy should be concerned with assisting individuals in constructing meaning through the naming and renaming of shared experience. Rorty portrays his work as building upon what Dewey offered some fifty years earlier, but, in spite of their many commonalities, their differences are significant. Of relevance here is Rorty's rather limited view of what philosophy can or should do. As we shall see in the next chapter, Dewey envisioned philosophers doing more than just "keeping the conversation going" in fostering the development of a democratic public.

For Rorty, edifying philosophers are "intentionally peripheral."[37] By their very nature, edifying philosophers are parasites feasting on dominant ideologies. Their intent is to bring to the surface the false or questionable assumptions underlying extant belief systems. Since no one has a God's eye view of the world, the best anyone can do is to help others see the fallacies that exist in any and all systems of belief. Using parables, fables, and aphorisms the edifying philosopher seeks to educate by helping others to learn from their own mistakes as well as from the mistakes of others.

This is a significant contribution, but is it enough? Is it possible for edifying philosophers to use their subjective knowledge of the past and present to reconstruct the future in some meaningful way? Rorty's characterization makes it unlikely that edifying philosophers will turn their artistic arsenal (poetry, literary criticism, fables, etc.) against the forces of the future in an attempt to reconstruct human civilization into a better, more humane place to live. Rorty suggests that edifying philosophers in sending "the conversation off in new directions" may spawn "new normal discourses, new sciences, new philosophical research programs, and thus new objective truths,"[38] but, Rorty insists, possible new directions should emerge only as "accidental byproducts" of edifying activities. According to Rorty, "edifying philosophers have to decry the very notion of having a view, while avoiding having a view about having views."[39]

It is here that Rorty parts company with Dewey's pragmatic view and succumbs to what Dewey refers to as either/or thinking. As Charles Taylor explains, "Rorty believes that one can jettison the old epistemological view without espousing another one."[40] Taylor questions the feasibility of having what Rorty describes as a "pragmatism without method," adding that "just trying to walk away from the old epistemology, without working out an alternative conception, seems paradoxically a formula for remaining trapped in it to some degree."[41] At their best, Rorty's edifying philosophers emulate Socratic teachers who foster improvement in individuals by helping them learn from past mistakes. At their worse, edifying philosophers, in failing to use the tools of their craft to offer possible visions of a better future, become apologists for the status quo. With these concerns in mind we turn now to a discussion of Rorty's views on the relationship of philosophy to democracy.

PUBLIC VS. PRIVATE:
RORTY ON DEMOCRACY AND PHILOSOPHY

In his introduction to a recent work, Rorty suggests that the good associated with our culture, presumably western culture, can just as easily be supported by what he calls solidarity as by some objectivist belief in an ultimate, transcendent reality. If one chooses solidarity over objectivity, then one abandons the quest for "mind-independent and language independent reality."[42] Embracing solidarity means that political questions take precedence over metaphysical and epistemological ones. Political questions like "what are limits of our community?" and "Has what we gained in solidarity cost us our ability to listen to outsiders who are suffering?" become more important than questions about our status as rational, political animals or over what is the optimum social structure for humankind to actualize their potential. Such political questions should, suggests Rorty, dominate the discourse in our democracies.

In suggesting that democracy takes precedence over philosophy, Rorty favors extending the Jeffersonian principle of religious freedom to broader, more philosophical concerns. In separating one's religious views from one's participation in and affiliation with the civic order, Jefferson suggested that religious preference was an individual or private matter that should have no bearing on an individual's public or social role. By removing theological questions from the civic, if not public, debate, Jefferson's principle allowed individuals from differing religious perspectives to find or create common ground on civic or public issues. For the purpose of democratic politics, religious or theological first principles were deemed irrelevant.

In making religion a private affair, Jefferson's principle of religious freedom ensured individuals the right to embrace the religious beliefs of their choice, thus promoting religious toleration among groups and individuals of different views. This Jeffersonian principle, when extended to make philosophical beliefs a private rather than a public affair, has contributed to the development of what Benjamin Barber identifies as a form of "thin democracy." Such a democracy is characterized by a passive citizenry more concerned with procedural guarantees of individual liberties than in a creative and active democratic public.

Since, according to John Rawls, "philosophy as the search for truth about an independent metaphysical and moral order cannot...provide a workable and shared basis for a political conception of justice in a democratic society," we should be content, suggests Rorty, with a societal structure grounded on "such settled convictions as the belief in religious toleration and the rejection of slavery."[43] Just as religious and theological first principles are insufficient and unnecessary for establishing a democratic social order, Rorty suggests that there are no philosophical first principles capable of or necessary for establishing such a society. "For purposes of social theory, we can," suggests Rorty, "put aside such topics as an ahistorical human nature, the nature of selfhood, the motive of moral behavior, and meaning of human life."[44] According to Rorty, these are as irrelevant to politics as, according to Jefferson, are "questions about the Trinity and about transubstantiation."[45] Just as Jefferson's advocacy of the separation of church and state promoted religious freedom, Rorty suggests that "staying on the surface, philosophically speaking"[46] promotes political freedom.

A democracy that fosters such political freedom is not unlike a family whose members avoid discussing controversial religious, political, or social issues out of fear that disagreement over such issues would sever the blood and familial ties that bind the family together. Perhaps, as Rorty suggests, it is shared experiences and culturally defined social commitments, not philosophical or religious beliefs, that create the family as a partially functioning whole. Still, if ignoring or superficially treating problematic issues of belief is necessary to maintain the familial bond, then how strong or viable can such a bond be?

Admittedly, many families function by keeping things on the surface, but is such superficiality the ideal? Is it not possible for families to achieve, however contingent and temporal, some common ground? Such common ground is elusive and can never be reified, but strong, viable families are continuously striving to create and recreate common ground.

Disagreements are inevitable, but strong families share a core of common values that enable them to tolerate and respect differences among those who make up the family. In analogous fashion a democratic community needs more than just procedural guarantees protecting and promoting individuality if that democracy is to sustain itself against internal and external challenges. For the community to grow and prosper, the individuals comprising such a democracy must strive to create and recreate some, albeit contingent and temporal, common ground. As suggested previously, it is questionable whether Rorty's edifying philosophy is up to the task of assisting members of a community in creating and continuously recreating such common ground.

Rorty agrees that such common ground is desirable, but he cautions against trying to do the impossible. In regards to a family's or community's attempt to create common ground, Rorty reminds us that "no description of how things are from a God's-eye point of view, no skyhook provided by some contemporary or yet-to-be-developed science, is going to free us from the contingency of having been acculturated as we were."[47] In seeking common ground to bind disparate communities or elements within a community together, "we should not," warns Rorty, "look for skyhooks, but for toeholds."[48] Rorty recognizes that his cautionary tone is criticized by some as a "counsel of despair, an apologia for the powers that be."[49] Rorty counters such criticism, suggesting that the activity of getting beyond our cultural setting or, in Nagel's terms, "climbing out of our own minds" is a "process of reformation and enlargement rather than revolution."[50]

Like Kafka's traveler, that is, our philosopher, modern human beings cannot step out of or above our cultural setting, but we can expand our horizon by entertaining new options, recasting past experiences in imaginative ways in search of possible and plausible solutions to the problems of the moment and future. According to Rorty we can never completely shed our "Western democratic skins when we encounter another culture and we should not try. All we should do is to get inside the inhabitants of that culture long enough to get some ideas of how we look to them, and whether they have any ideas we can use."[51] Dewey emphasized the role that education could play in fostering this "reformation," but Rorty suggests that "our best chance for transcending our acculturation is to be brought up in a culture which prides itself on *not* being monolithic—on its willingness to listen to neighboring cultures."[52] What about those brought up in a more monolithic culture? What, if anything, can and should be done to foster and sustain these cultures tolerant of others? Rorty has little to say in response to these questions.

From a Deweyian perspective, it is here that education and philosophy merge; where educative experiences create this sense of solidarity, the reformed democratic community that Rorty advocates. Such a community is clearly Rorty's goal, but he is not clear what role, if any, philosophy and education can or should play in creating such a community. Other than suggesting that as edifying philosophers, novelists, journalists, and poets are better suited to foster such reformation than modern philosophers, he has little to say regarding achieving this goal. Though seemingly sharing a common goal, Rorty's tone is noticeably different from Dewey's. In explaining in clear and readable prose the fallacies of modern philosophical thought, Rorty provides an invaluable service. Beyond this he is silent. He offers no real plan for reconstructing that which he and others have so effectively undermined. To borrow a phrase often used by Marxist and other radicals in condemnation of liberal philosophers, Rorty is a parlor pink, that is, one who understands and articulates the mistakes and injustices of the past and present, but contributes little to correcting these injustices.

As noted earlier, it has been suggested that Rorty's championing of liberal democracy amounts to little more than support of an unjust status quo. In response, Rorty suggests that "there is nothing wrong with liberal democracy, nor with the philosophers who have tried to enlarge its scope." Furthermore, adds Rorty, there is "nothing wrong with the hopes of the Enlightenment, the hopes which created western democracies."[53] Rorty opposes any efforts by realists or anyone else who tries to reify these hopes into some form of objective truth, but as the creations of the human mind, these hopes have proven their utility over the centuries. Still if liberal democracy is, as Benjamin Barber argues, a "thin" theory of democracy, then from a Deweyian perspective, there is something wrong with these Enlightenment hopes.

According to Barber, liberal democracy is "one whose democratic values are prudential and thus provisional, optional, and conditional—means to exclusively individualistic and private ends."[54] Such a democratic form of government "can never rise far above the provisional and private prudence expressed in John Locke's explanation that men consent to live under government only for 'the mutual preservation of their lives, liberties, and estates.'"[55] This "thin" version of democracy "is concerned more to promote individual liberty than to secure public justice, to advance interest rather than to discover goods, and to keep men safely apart rather than to bring them together."[56] From this perspective, liberal democracy is less concerned with finding or creating common ground than it is in ensuring that the private rights of individuals are maintained.

It is unlikely that Rorty would embrace this characterization of liberal democracy as "at best a politics of static interests, never a politics of transformation: a politics of bargaining and exchange, never a politics of invention and creation; and a politics that conceives of women and men at their worst (in order to protect them from themselves), never at their potential best (to help them become better than they are)."[57] Rorty characterizes the bourgeois liberal cultures of western democracies as more dynamic, as "constantly adding on more windows, constantly enlarging its sympathies."[58] Still, in advocating the separation of personal religious, philosophical, or social convictions from the public or political realm, Rorty's view of democracy is closer to this "thin" democracy than to the "strong" democracy that Barber favors as an alternative.

Rorty speaks with pride of our (presumably Western democratic) culture's reliance on the mechanics of procedural justice in handling sticky moral and legal problems. Since no one has a God's eye view of such matters, our best hope is to rely on the practices of procedural justice that have evolved over time and, through trial and error, proven their effectiveness. While certainly not perfect, Rorty suggests that reliance on such procedural practice has proven to be far superior to resolving disputes than appealing to competing and conflicting religious or philosophical beliefs. Giving the technically trained specialist his due, Rorty explains that "we do not want doctors to differentiate between the values of the lives they are saving, any more than we want defense lawyers to worry too much about the innocence of clients, or teachers to worry about which students will make the best of the education they are offering."[59]

Since no human can answer the larger philosophical questions implied in each of the previous situations, the best we can do is to muddle through, relying upon procedures that have been developed and revised over time. Once again, staying on the surface philosophically has become a necessity for modern, technically complex societies. Perhaps it is the ultimate irony that Rorty, in championing modern Western societies as embodiments of what is right with Enlightenment thought, embraces the professional, the technically trained expert, in all areas but in philosophy itself. According to Rorty, moral progress owes "more to the specialists in particularity—historians, novelists, ethnographers, and muckraking journalists, for example—than to such specialists in universality as theologians and philosophers."[60]

Rorty is on target in cautioning us against philosophers' tendency to seek the "God's eye view," but philosophers in Rorty's scheme have but two choices. In refusing to turn their energies toward reconstructing the future, philosophers become either cynics convinced that human progress is impossible or playful amateurs, content with identifying the absurdities of our modern existence. Rorty favors the latter role, but in either case philosophy is impotent, incapable of inspiring humankind to create a better future.

POSTMODERNISM'S IMPOTENCE IN EFFECTING EDUCATIONAL CHANGE

Inspiring the creation of better, more humane worlds is education's reason to be. As Beyer and Liston note, Rorty and other postmodernists offer little for educators "for whom both intellectual engagement and transformative practice are mandatory."[61] Beyer and Liston suggest that postmodernists, including Rorty, go too far in their distrust of metanarratives. The belief that any coherent system of thought must inevitably develop into an intellectual strait jacket has led, especially on moral issues, to an overemphasis on local or cultural perspectives. Such ethnocentrism, to use Rorty's term, is shortsighted for "local efforts frequently require insight attainable only through the examination and critique of non-local sources of exploitation and oppression, and necessitate directions that are ascertainable through cultural and moral visions that may transcend the immediate situation."[62] Once again embracing one need not cancel out the other. Reminiscent of Beck's argument discussed in an earlier chapter for a more inclusive view of educational philosophy, Beyer and Liston suggest that local and global perspectives can be used to complement and supplement one another. Suggesting that postmodernism "draws too sharp a distinction between the local and the more distant," Beyer and Liston argue "for a more dialectical relationship between these things: the sense that the local can illuminate the more general, and that the global can heighten our sensitivity to the more particular."[63]

Many postmodernists, most notably Foucault, "emphasize a concern for the 'other'—those who have been oppressed or exploited."[64] Once again this highly commendable interest in ensuring that the heretofore excluded voices be heard "has led some postmodernists to become suspicious of or hostile to 'community.'"[65] History has shown us that oppression and exploitation have often occurred in the name of the collective, but are communities necessarily oppressive and constraining? In opting for procedural guarantees to ensure that the voices of others will be heard, Rorty and others clearly demonstrate their fear of the tyranny of the community. The desire for the "other" to be heard is commendable, but unless it is accompanied by or includes a compelling vision of some legitimate, albeit contingent and temporal, common ground, expanding and continuing the conversation becomes a hollow objective.

If educators see themselves as change agents, as involved in transforming society from what it is into what it should be, then such an activity requires a compelling vision of what should be. Their emphasis on local and regional perspectives and their suspicions of community prevent postmodernists from providing or offering such a vision. Postmodernists have appropriately deconstructed the belief systems of the modern world, but more than deconstruction is needed. As Cherryholmes suggests, "both constructors and deconstructors are needed."[66] In their inability or unwillingness to offer a vision of what should replace the system that they so effectively undermined, postmodernist thinkers abandoned the philosopher's role of mediating between the past and present. In focusing all their energies in combating the fallacies of the past, postmodernists rendered themselves impotent in the equally significant task of recreating the present and future. For this reason, as we shall see in the next chapter, Rorty and other postmodernists are not, as they claim, the legitimate heirs of the pragmatic tradition created by John Dewey and others.

Philosophy _as_ Education: Reviving Dewey's Vision

In 1945, John Dewey learned that Jack Lamb, "a young man of intelligence, promise, and sincerity," had followed his advice and decided to study sociology rather than philosophy. Praising his choice, Dewey wrote, "I'm glad you are going into sociology, not into professional philosophy. You will use philosophy which is more than many professionals do."[1] This statement reflects Dewey's growing frustration with professional philosophers' unwillingness to address the pressing public problems of the day. It also demonstrates Dewey's appreciation for the importance of historical and social understanding in the reconstruction of the future in any meaningful way. Dewey's affinity for the sciences is well known, but it is history, not science, that commanded most of his attention. History, suggests Dewey, when properly taught, is "the most effective conscious tool" for moral instruction. History, taught not as a body of facts but as "indirect sociology" and imbued with a philosophical orientation, enabled students "to appreciate the values of social life, to see in imagination the forces which favor men's effective cooperation with one another, to understand the sorts of character that help and hold back."[2]

Dewey's notion that serious young men would use philosophy more in the study and application of "indirect sociology" than professional philosophers do suggests that something was seriously amiss with his chosen field. As we shall see, Dewey's conceptualization of philosophy is dramatically different from the professionalized version of it (see chapter 4) that had come to dominate academic philosophy. Following a brief sketch of the life and thought of John Dewey, Dewey's vision of what philosophy should be and do is explained. In this context, philosophy's role in fostering democracy is discussed, along with its intimate connection to education. In suggesting that philosophers must understand the past in order to help humankind build a better future, Dewey's vision is offered as an appropriate response to Kafka's fable introduced in the previous chapter. In this context, comparisons to the thought of Richard Rorty and other postmodernists are made. The chapter concludes with suggestions for constructing a new educational philosophy which has the ultimate goal of fostering the development of what Dewey calls "the Great Community."

DEWEY'S LIFE AND THOUGHT

Born in 1859—the same year that Horace Mann died and that saw the publication of Charles Darwin's *Origins of the Species*—Dewey lived through the Civil War, two world wars, the Great Depression, and numerous lesser conflicts, and died as the Cold War emerged full blown on the global scene. During his lifetime, the United States was transformed from a largely agrarian, experimental republic into the major industrial and military power in the world. Growing up in Puritan New England, Dewey gradually abandoned his religious foundations, moving as he explains "From Absolutism to Experimentalism." Attaining his undergraduate degree from the University of Vermont and eventually his Ph.D. from Johns Hopkins University, Dewey retained his religious commitment during his professorship at the University of Michigan in the 1880s and 1890s. As a young man Dewey embraced the "Social Gospel" movement as a means of connecting his commitment to democracy to an absolutist metaphysics—Hegelian idealism.

His commitment to social justice and democratic principles never waned, but by the early 1890s, Dewey had begun to distance himself from other-worldly metaphysics. Upon moving to Chicago in 1894 to chair the Department of Philosophy, Psychology, and Pedagogy at the University of Chicago, Dewey stopped participating in religious activities. By this time he had transformed his metaphysical idealism into pragmatic naturalism. Finally, feeling comfortable that his commitment to democratic principles could be sustained by grounding them in experience, Dewey spent much of the remainder of his life working out the implications of this philosophical shift for his social, political, and educational ideas.

The years that Dewey lived in Chicago were productive ones. Here, he continued his commitment to social justice by working with Jane Addams at Hull House, experiencing firsthand the dehumanizing effects that America's transformation into an industrialized and urbanized oligarchy produced. Here too, Dewey established his famous "Lab School," a living, self-correcting community, as a testing ground for his evolving educational ideas. Here he emerged, along with William James and Charles S. Pierce, as a founder of that uniquely American brand of philosophy known as pragmatism.

Leaving Chicago in 1904, Dewey assumed a professorship of philosophy at Columbia University in New York City, a position held until his retirement in 1929. In addition to teaching, writing, and numerous other academic responsibilities, Dewey struggled to find ways to construct "The Great Community" and to make the world "safe for democracy." Initially supportive of Wilson's war policy—for which his former student, Randolph Bourne, criticized him for falling "prey to the very mistakes his philosophy was designed to prevent"³—Dewey participated in the quixotic "Outlaw War" movement during the postwar period. During these years and throughout his life,

Dewey was the most important advocate of participatory democracy, that is of the belief that democracy as an ethical ideal calls upon men and women to build communities in which the necessary opportunities and resources are available for every individual to fully realize his or her particular capacities and powers through participation in political, social, and cultural life.⁴

Though officially retired, Dewey remained remarkably active during the last twenty-three years of his life. He continued his prolific writing, publishing major works on aesthetics, religion, politics, education, logic, and epistemology. He remained active in social causes, including traveling to Mexico to chair the Commission of Inquiry investigating the charges leveled against Leon Trotsky. In 1946 John Dewey remarried a woman almost half his age and with her adopted two Belgian war orphans.⁵ He died in 1952.

As suggested earlier, Dewey was a prolific scholar throughout his life. He published scores of books and pamphlets, hundreds of articles for scholarly and popular journals and magazines, and gave innumerable speeches and lectures—public as well as academic—on topics ranging from Hegelian metaphysics to woman's suffrage. Indeed, it is not an exaggeration to suggest that from 1900 to 1940, Dewey published more each year than many small college faculties produced during all of these years. Unfortunately, Dewey did not always write well. In the words of Justice Oliver Wendell Holmes, "Dewey writes as the creator would write, if he were intent on explaining all of his creation but was hopelessly inarticulate." Dewey's works are often misunderstood, but more frequently Dewey is not read. As John Novak explains, "John Dewey is like the Bible—often alluded to (both by his supporters and detractors) but seldom read ..."[6]

In attempting to grasp the essentials of Dewey's thought, one could easily be overwhelmed by the sheer volume of it. For those brave or foolish enough to dive into one of Dewey's works, they are likely to find his prose stiff and lacking in imagination. In addition, while there is an abundance of literature about Dewey, much of it treats him either as a saint or a villain. Dewey, as Westbrook's recent excellent biography demonstrates, is neither. Since his death, as during much of his life, Dewey continues to be both honored and condemned. Both reviled and praised as the so-called founder of progressive education, Dewey is often thought of as the founder of all things good (and bad) in American education.

Whether due to not reading or not understanding Dewey's works, there is a tendency to associate his life and thought with various and sometimes conflicting labels. It is ironic that one who was so opposed to either/or thinking elicited, all too often, an either/or reaction from many people. Perhaps as his life and thought becomes better known, through the work of Westbrook, Rorty, and others, he will be increasingly recognized as a complex thinker whose thought could never be captured by any reductionist label. This chapter seeks to contribute to such recognition and to whet the reader's appetite for more information about this remarkable figure in American thought. If this chapter is successful, in addition to gaining insights into where educational philosophy is, has been, and ought to be, readers will be motivated to further investigate both the man and his thought.

In concluding this overview of the life and thought of one of America's preeminent philosophers, a brief discussion of Dewey's *Experience and Education* is offered. Such a discussion is appropriate, since in this little volume Dewey provides us with his most concise and readable statement of his position on the relationships among philosophy, democracy, and education. Since Dewey understood the intimate connection between philosophy and education, his position is of significance for us here as we search for insights regarding where and what educational philosophy ought to be.

In *Experience and Education*, written in 1937, Dewey reiterates his opposition to either/or thinking. Specifically, Dewey rejects the either/ or (Platonic/Aristotelian) world view that dominated the Western world for so long. From this rather traditional perspective, knowledge is either innate, that is, inside the individual at birth awaiting the right pneumonic device to bring it to consciousness; or external to human beings awaiting our discovery. In either case, an absolute is implied, resulting in the imposition of knowledge and values upon each new generation. Dewey suggests that such a world view may be appropriate for a monarchy or some other form of autocracy, but it is antithetical to education in a democracy.

Is rejection enough? Is the urge to destroy really—as Bakunin suggests—a creative urge? Dewey realizes that if the so-called "new education" is developed as a negative reaction to traditional beliefs, then its advocates have fallen into the trap of either/or thinking. All too often what occurred in Dewey's name and under the rubric of progressivism was nothing more than mere reaction to the authorities of the past, with little or no attempt to reconstruct that which had been torn down. While such deconstruction may be necessary, it is not sufficient. For Dewey, a vision of a better way is needed, that is, a plan for reconstruction based on a vision of what should and could be.

Dewey suggests that many so-called progressives built their "new education" as a negative reaction to that which they did not like or with which they did not agree. Rather than just rebelling against the traditional version of either/or thinking, Dewey based his "new education" on experience. In distinguishing good or educative experiences from bad or miseducative experiences, Dewey suggests, that a good experience is characterized by both interaction and continuity. To Dewey, reality was neither innate nor outside the human being, but the sum total of experiences constructed by humans as they interacted with an ever changing world.

An educative experience is one in which an active mind interacts with a wide open world in order to solve genuine problems that are continuous with, yet different from, that individual's previous knowledge or experience. Human beings are creatures of habit, and habitual behavior is necessary for continuity in our lives. Still, habitual behavior is not sufficient. For humans to grow or learn, they must encounter problematic situations. Once the problem is recognized, possible hypotheses or plans for action, derivative of but going beyond past experiences, are developed. Each possible hypothesis is analyzed in an attempt to anticipate likely consequences. Keeping in mind that the most desirable plan of action is one that fosters long-term growth, humans eventually choose a plan, act

on it, and then evaluate it to determine if it produced the desired consequences. While it is not possible to predict with absolute certainty the
consequences of a particular plan of action, analysis of past experiences
enables human beings to be more than just pawns in the never-ending
process of evolution.

It is the ability to do more than just react to external stimuli—that
is, to think and reflect before acting, to respond intelligently to a problematic situation requiring more than a mere habitual reaction—that distinguishes humans from less intelligent animals. Based then on this view
of experience, Dewey concludes that the educator's role is one of creating problems for students to solve, problems that demand more of
humans than mere habitual behavior.

In addition to offering a concise theory of experience, Dewey's
Experience and Education offers insights into Dewey's view of democracy. True to form, democracy was, for Dewey, more than just opposition
to authoritarian rule. Dewey was no anarchist. The basis for authority in
a democracy is experience. Dewey suggests that in a true democracy, "it
is not the will or desire of any one person (a philosopher-king or scien-
tist) which establishes order, but the moving spirit of the whole group."[7]
Creating and sustaining such a "moving spirit" is, as we shall see, what
education and philosophy should be about.

WHAT IS PHILOSOPHY?

The key to understanding this intimate relationship between philosophy and education can be found in the term "philosophy" itself.
Literally meaning the love of wisdom, Dewey explains that "Whenever
philosophy has been taken seriously, it has always been assumed that it
signified achieving a wisdom which would influence the conduct of life."[8]
Though facts may be helpful, wisdom moves beyond worldly facts to a
general attitude or disposition about the world. Wisdom so defined is not
a fixed entity that once found is to be applied routinely to all of life's
questions, but a disposition or habit of seeking and creating connections
among the disparate aspects of life. Philosophy, viewed in this way, loses
its elitism and professional status. As we shall see (in the next chapter), it
becomes an activity that even children can and should do. As Dewey
explains "any person who is open-minded and sensitive to new perceptions, and who has concentration in connecting them has, in so far, a
philosophic disposition."[9]

In attempting to describe what philosophy is and is not, Dewey struggles with what he characterizes as the "first and last problem for a student of philosophy: The problem of what after all is the business and province of philosophy itself."[10] In characterizing philosophy as a love of wisdom, Dewey cautions against associating wisdom with the Platonic use of the word. Wisdom, "whatever it is, is not," for Dewey, "a mode of science or knowledge."[11] For Dewey, and he suggests, for any serious student of the field, philosophy should be perceived as an "intellectualized wish, an aspiration subjected to rational discriminations and tests, a social hope, reduced to a working program of action, a prophecy of the future, but one disciplined by serious thought and knowledge."[12]

Conceived of as an intellectualized wish, as a rational aspiration, philosophy becomes a moral enterprise. From this perspective, wisdom is not a fixed entity, but "as a moral term it refers to a choice about something to be done, a preference for living this sort of life rather than that. It refers not to accomplished reality but to a desired future which our desires, when translated into articulate conviction, may help bring into existence."[13] There are rational elements in this "desired future," but philosophy as the love of wisdom is more than a rational activity.

If philosophy is more concerned about "basic beliefs about the sort of life to be lived" than about an objective analysis of some ultimate reality, then the question becomes what are the sources of those basic beliefs. The inclination toward one way of life over another originates, suggests Dewey, not in science or in a purely intellectualized arena, but in "certain systematized predilections and aversions"[14] fostered by the institutions and customs of the culture we inhabit. In short, these inclinations or predilections are derived from our collective experiences—experiences resulting from our ancestors' attempts to understand their world and transmit that understanding in some meaningful way to each subsequent generation. Ultimately this inclination or preference for a particular way of life is the product of human beings reconstructing their experiences and determining over time which experiences produce the most positive outcomes. The development of such preferences can be chronicled through the evolution of human intelligence as humankind developed the ability to do more than just react to various external stimuli affecting their lives.

Since the stimuli varied over time and place, there emerged various cultures and varied intellectual temperaments as human beings struggled to create meaning out of their own particular social and physical phenomena. Dewey suggests that this has resulted in various politics, literature, arts, and even philosophies as manifestations of diverse human culture. For this reason, it is reasonable, suggests Dewey, to associate various philosophical temperaments with particular cultures or societies. For example, it makes sense, Dewey suggests, to speak of German, French, English, or even American philosophies for each, having emerged from these cultures, is distinct and represents "different ways of construing life."[15]

To further illustrate this point, Dewey predicted some sixty-five years ago that when women begin to write philosophy, their perspective or temperament will be dramatically different from the male-dominated perspectives that had and continue to dominate the field. One has only to look at the growing influence that feminist thought is having on both philosophy and educational philosophy to appreciate the wisdom of Dewey's comment.

The point to all of this is to suggest that since there is no single, absolute reality, there can be no correct system or method of philosophy. That being the case, we seem to be back again to the question "What is philosophy?" If there is no ultimate philosophical truth or method, one wonders if there is any common characteristic of this entity known as philosophy. In response to this query, Dewey answers in the affirmative suggesting that the common element in all human intelligence is the ability and inclination, to borrow Bruner's phrase, to go beyond the information given. This forward-looking capacity is, suggests Dewey, the mark of intelligence, a creative intelligence capable of determining that which is desirable in the past and present and using it to create a better vision of the future.[16] In a later section, this ability to use an understanding of the past and present to create a more positive future will be discussed in more detail. For now it is time to discuss how this forward-looking characteristic has been fostered in the past and how this original understanding of philosophy may help us in reestablishing the intimate connection between philosophy and education.

Dewey suggests that this forward-looking, philosophic disposition can be characterized as a "power to learn, or to extract meaning, from even the unpleasant vicissitudes of experience and to embody what is learned in an ability to go on learning..."[17] Dewey is not suggesting that wisdom can only or can best be achieved through painful experiences, but uses the Stoic tradition to illustrate how the philosophic disposition demands that one seek or create meaning even in less than desirable circumstances. In one in which this philosophic disposition has taken root, superficial explanations or surface understandings are no longer acceptable. In this view, philosophy, as the "power to learn," is never content with the isolated event; it seeks to place such experiences in context realizing that only in context is anything meaningful.

The assertion that philosophy, in any meaningful sense, and education are one raises eyebrows today, but the Greeks of ancient Athens would have understood. It is here, Dewey tells us, that philosophy, as we use the word today, emerged. It emerged as the Sophists, the first professional educators, charged with instructing the youth in virtue, began asking educational questions: questions such as what is virtue and can it be taught? what is the relationship between virtue and knowledge and what constitutes knowledge? and how is knowledge taught and learned? Within two or three generations after the Sophists began raising such educational questions, philosophy abandoned its educational and practical roots. Rather than being seen as a "power to learn" about the world and how to make it better, philosophy came to mean pure reason as humankind's highest calling. In short, philosophy became an end "in itself" creating a gulf between pure philosophy and its educational origins that has only rarely been spanned. Nonetheless "the fact that the stream of European (Western) philosophical thought arose as a theory of educational procedure remains an eloquent witness to the intimate connection of philosophy and education."[18]

Dewey suggests that what was true for the Athenians is just as true for us today. Now, as then, "philosophic problems arise because of widespread and widely felt difficulties in social practice."[19] This reality is often disguised, Dewey continues, because philosophers have become a professional class using a technical language different from the vocabulary of those confronting the difficulty directly. Perhaps it is possible for the professional to analyze such difficulties in the abstract, but to remain so "pure" is to deny this intimate connection between educational problems and philosophic thought. Furthermore, if such philosophizing has any significance, it will be determined through education, "the laboratory in which philosophic distinctions become concrete and are tested."[20]

Students of philosophy "in itself" sometimes mistakenly think of philosophy "as so much nimble or severe intellectual exercise," but, when and if they are helped to see its educational origins, their philosophical inquiry is enriched, enabling it to penetrate beyond the technical to the human side of the problem. Attending to the connections between educational problems and philosophic thought makes for better, more relevant philosophy, for as Dewey explains, "if a theory makes no difference in educational endeavors, it must be artificial. The educational point of view enables one to envisage the philosophic problems where they arise and thrive, where they are at home, and where acceptance or rejection makes a difference in practice."[21]

Perhaps it is the ultimate irony that the branch of philosophy most closely associated with John Dewey rejected his vision of philosophy. Dewey resisted the notion that philosophy was "some sort of super-science," or "...foundational discipline of culture..." To Dewey, philosophy should not be a search for certainty, but an attempt "to gain critical perspective, to locate, specify, and clarify human problems..."[22] From this perspective, educational philosophy is neither philosophy *of* education nor philosophy *and* education. Certainly it is not just a branch or subset of a larger philosophical system or tradition. Implicit in Dewey's vision is the idea that philosophy and education are one. For as Dewey suggests, "if we are willing to conceive of education as the forming of fundamental disposition.... philosophy may even be defined as the general theory of education.[23] James Giarelli and others characterize this Deweyian vision as philosophy *as* education.

DEWEY'S DEMOCRATIC VISION

The rejection of Dewey's perspective of philosophy *as* education contributed to the demise of public philosophy in America. In addition, Dewey suggests that professional philosophers must shoulder some of the responsibility for our society's (in his day and ours) failure to develop a genuinely democratic public. Dewey speaks to these concerns in *The Public and Its Problems*, written in response to Walter Lippman's criticism of democracy. While Dewey rivals Lippman in itemizing voter ignorance and apathy, Dewey goes further by offering us a vision of what democracy can and should be. According to Dewey, the problem lies not in an inherent weakness of democracy or human nature, but in our institutions' failure to promote democracy. This failure, suggests Dewey, stems in part from our founding fathers' rather limited vision of what democracy could or should be.

Our founding fathers, in creating a republic based on an individual's inalienable rights, committed a grave error. Declaring hostility against tyranny in all its forms, Jefferson and the founding fathers' vision of democracy emerged as a reaction against an oppressive form of government. While such a reaction is understandable, it culminated in a general fear of government and "a desire to reduce it to a minimum so as to limit the evil it could do."[24]

Though couched in positive terms like democracy and freedom, the founding fathers' vision centered on protecting the inalienable or natural rights of the individual. Such a protectionist theory of government found a ready ally in individualism, "a theory which endowed singular persons in isolation from any associations except those which were deliberately formed for their own ends, with native or natural rights."[25] Unfortunately in an attempt to justify their revolt against an abusive government, the founding fathers embraced both protectionism and individualism in order to justify their casting off the yoke of British imperialism. As translated by Jefferson, this Lockean doctrine of the inalienable rights of humankind became the justification for limiting the power of governments to sustaining and protecting such individual rights as "life, liberty and the pursuit of happiness."

This negative reaction to the British monarchy and the ecclesiastic and feudal traditions associated with it—while understandable, even commendable—was, nonetheless, unfortunate. Unfortunate, because it resulted in thinking of government as the enemy—as a many-headed tyrant awaiting any and all opportunities to take away our cherished individual freedoms. Accompanying this fear of governmental tyranny was an equally powerful belief that individuals are often weak and easily tempted to encroach on another's "activities and properties."[26]

This ambivalent, if not paradoxical view of government provided the foundation for the development of what Barber refers to as "weak democracy." From this incident of our founding fathers falling prey to either/or thinking has evolved modern forms of constitutional democracy such as a complex system of checks and balances among the branches of government, representatives—both legislative and executive—elected by majority vote, and general, if not universal suffrage. While many of these "democratic" institutions have had a very positive legacy, they have also obstructed the use of government as an instrument for the creation of a genuine democratic public. Rather than assisting us in finding or creating common ground among disparate individuals and groups, our republican form of government has fostered separateness and individuality—not genuine democratic community.

Genuine—what Benjamin Barber calls "strong"—democracy consists of democratic procedure that "changes people and their beliefs, transforming I's into We."[27] This obstructionist legacy remains the norm, and Dewey's suggestion that "the democratic public is still largely inchoate and unorganized"[28] is just as accurate a portrayal of contemporary democracies as it was of democracies in 1927.

People are, Dewey suggests, "capable of being democratic."[29] They are not, by nature, irrational and antisocial. Since all behavior is learned, there is no reason why cooperative and experimental behavior cannot be acquired. The role of the philosopher is to foster such behavior by contributing to the creation of an environment in which the habits that a democracy needs can develop. Rather than continuing a misguided quest for certainty or for the most desirable forms of social organization, philosophers should, suggests Dewey, lead the way in "the search for conditions under which the Great Society may become the Great Community. When these conditions are brought into being they will create their own forms."[30]

What are these conditions that need to be fulfilled for Dewey's ideal state or public—his Great Community—to come into existence? In search of an answer to that question, Dewey's views of human nature, his concept of freedom, and his ideas on democracy are discussed. Suggesting that humans, like many other animals, are by nature social creatures, Dewey distinguishes this organic need for association from the establishment of community. As Dewey puts it, "associated activity needs no explanation; things are made that way..."[31] but communities are purposeful creations involving intelligent and moral choices. Such communities came into being as humankind developed the ability to anticipate likely consequences of particular associations and to value some associations more than others.

In creating communities, in showing preference for certain kinds of associations, individual human beings make choices based upon their unique life histories and their capacity for intelligent foresight. Inherent within each individual is the potential or capacity for development. How that potential manifests itself depends upon that individual's "distinctive way of feeling the impacts of the world and of showing a preferential bias in response to these impacts..."[32] The point to be made here is that Dewey considered human potentiality and freedom to be much more complex than the inalienable or natural rights view posited by Locke and embraced by our founding fathers. These classical liberals assumed that "individuals have such native and original endowment of rights, powers, and wants that all that is required on the side of institutions and laws is to eliminate the obstructions they offer to the free play of the natural equipment of individuals."[33] While Dewey believed that individuals could and should reconstruct the world they found themselves in, he also believed that the nature of the institutions or human constructions the individual encountered defined to some degree the kind of choices available to each individual. In short, the nature of the previously constructed communities that individuals find themselves in plays a significant role in determining to what extent an individual's capacity for development is achieved.

For Dewey, associating freedom with specific inalienable rights was overly simplistic and too restrictive. Freedom for Dewey meant releasing and fulfilling the unique potentialities that each individual possesses. As social beings, this potential is best released or more fully achieved through interaction with others, and the quality of that interaction is dependent upon the quality of the communities individuals inhabit. For Dewey, it is the democratic community that is best suited for releasing the potentialities of each individual.

The Great Community equates with Dewey's vision of what democracy ought to be, but in making this association, it should be noted that the ideal community means more than a democratic form of government. For Dewey, the idea of democracy should be exemplified by the state, but genuine democracy "must affect all modes of human association, the family, the school, industry, religion."[34] All of us belong to many groups, and our associations within these groups should develop and grow over time. But Dewey suggests, for the Great Community to come into existence, these associations need to "interact flexibly and fully in connection with other groups." Some groups are better suited than others for fostering this kind of interaction and for promoting the growth of individuals' potential. For example, a member of a group of bank robbers may develop proficiency in the skills required for such a vocation, and may develop strong bonds of friendship and loyalty among members of this group, but "only at the cost of repression of those potentialities which can be realized only through membership in other groups."[35] Since the robber cannot interact as easily or as flexibly with others, belonging to such a group tends to isolate its members and thus limit or impede the development of their potential. In contrast, membership in familial, scientific, and other democratic social groups increases the likelihood of participants developing their potential and enriching their lives. The ideal group should empower individuals to develop their potential by facilitating full and flexible interaction with individuals in other groups and as part of a larger community.

As a "mode of associated life,"[36] democracy may be characterized as a self-corrective community of inquiry. Dewey's vision of democracy as a self-corrective community of inquiry expands upon his notion of scientific community where the norms of inquiry are both accepted and continually challenged. While there is no perfect mode of association, democracy "has a greater capacity for self-correction and growth than any other human arrangements (to date)."[37] A democratic form of associate living must never be reified; it "requires the acceptance of shared values that are at once stable and flexible, and not tolerance but encouragement of public criticism."[38] Democracy, for Dewey, constitutes his moral vision, his "belief in the ability of human experience to generate the aims and methods by which further experience will grow in ordered richness."[39]

As individuals become human, as they learn that communities are experimental and that they can and should contribute to their development or demise, the seeds of democracy are planted. To aid in this development of genuine democracy, that is, to assist every individual in learning how to become human, is the task of philosophy. As such, the major problem for the philosopher is communication, that is, making possible for the public at large to "acquire knowledge of those conditions that have created it and how these conditions affect the values of associated life."[40] To effect this kind of communication, "presentation is fundamentally important and presentation is a question of art." The philosopher must communicate with the masses. If technical or high-brow language is used, the philosopher communicates only with those technically high-brow. The philosopher, in helping the masses to discover that even the most common things offer insights into the human condition, is an artist. While communicating with the masses has largely been ignored by the professional philosopher, poets, novelists, and playwrights have demonstrated that "the problem of presentation is not insoluble."[41] As an educator, the philosopher must use the tools of the artists to empower the people to create a democratic society. In short, the philosopher must master the art of presentation.

Presentation is an essential aspect of communication, but there are other, suggests Dewey, equally important areas that must not be neglected. An equally essential need "is the improvement of the methods and conditions of debate, discussion, and persuasion."[42] If democracy is to survive and improve, progress must be made not only in the presentation of new knowledge as it is discovered and created, but also in the processes of inquiry that lead to the creation and/or discovery of this new knowledge. Progress, not in perfecting, but in improving both the procedures by which knowledge is obtained and disseminated, is essential if a truly democratic public is to be achieved. While investigations into those procedures may require expertise, "it is not," suggests Dewey, "necessary that the many should have the knowledge and skill to carry on the needed investigations," but everyone must "have the ability to judge of the bearing of the knowledge supplied by others upon common concerns."[43] Once again, Dewey favors thinking of the philosopher not as an expert who frames and executes policy, but as a wise amateur capable of assisting in the discovery and dissemination of the procedures through which the masses can frame and execute policy.

Finally, Dewey's discussion of the local community merits consideration. Since, as Dewey suggests, "democracy must begin at home, and its home is the neighborly community,"[44] philosophers should ground their investigations in the conditions which affect human associations at the local level and design their presentations to address a particular local community. For, as Dewey notes, "unless local community life can be restored," there is little chance of a truly democratic society emerging.

In analyzing the importance of presentation—including a call for the improvement of the conditions and methods of debate, discussion and persuasion—and in advocating renewed attention to the local community, Dewey was clearly ahead of his time. Recognizing that democracy as it was currently fashioned and practiced in the United States between the two world wars was in serious trouble, Dewey suggested that the solution to the problems of democracy was more democracy. In this discussion of what he characterizes as "The Problem of Method," Dewey anticipated Benjamin Barber's 1984 work, *Strong Democracy*. Reminiscent of Dewey, Barber suggests that "democracy breeds democracy,"[45] and goes on to offer a significantly Deweyian vision of what political democracy ought to be and specific proposals for operationalizing this vision.

Dewey's attention to the art of presentation suggests that the goal of education and of the philosopher as educator in genuine democracies is to share information and skills in such a way as to enable the ordinary citizen to attain the skills and knowledge needed for participation in democratic institutions. Unlike liberal modes of democracy—the kind Rorty embraces and that Barber refers to as weak or thin—"strong democracy is the politics of amateurs, where every man is compelled to encounter every other man without the intermediary of expertise."[46] It is by mastering the art of presentation and by creating appropriate condition and methods for facilitating democratic talk that philosophers contribute to the development of such citizens. As Barber explains, without such citizens there can be no genuine democracy.[47]

Describing voting in contemporary democracies as "rather like using a public toilet,"[48] that is, something we do in private and rarely discuss in public, Barber argues that "strong democracy requires unmediated self-government by an engaged citizenry."[49] For this to occur institutions must be created at the local, regional, and national levels, that "involve individuals...in common talk, common decision-making and political judgement, and common action."[50]

Such talk and action requires specific skills and dispositions not common to thin democracies or other forms of social organization. For example, talk in a strong democracy involves listening as well as speaking, but listening takes on special characteristics. As Barber explains, "I will listen means to the strong democrat not that I will scan my adversary's position for weaknesses and potential trade-offs, nor even(...) that I will tolerantly permit him to say whatever he chooses. It means, rather, I will put myself in his place, I will listen for a common rhetoric evocative of a common purpose or a common good."[51]

Dewey refers to enhancing such skills and dispositions of democratic talk as the "problem of method." It is in creating the conditions which foster the development of these democratic skills and dispositions that the philosopher can and should contribute to the creation and sustainment of strong democracies. Building upon the framework Dewey offered in 1927, Barber provides us with concrete proposals for transforming our contemporary "thin" or weak democracies into political structures more compatible with Dewey's vision. In developing a twelve-point, strong democratic program for the revitalization of citizenship—including but not limited to the establishment of a national system of neighborhood assemblies; a two-stage initiative and referendum process that requires deliberation and reflection of those participating in the process; and public sponsorship of common work and common action through local volunteer programs[52]—Barber goes beyond Dewey in suggesting plausible solutions to the problem of method. While these practical solutions involve the schools only indirectly as one of many social institutions responsible for the creation of the associative form of living known as democracy, they are educative solutions. They take as their collective goal the development of an engaged citizenry capable of embracing, creating, and sustaining democratic institutions.

As this section draws to a close, it is time to make explicit the intimate connection between education, philosophy, and democracy. As noted earlier, Dewey once defined philosophy as "the general theory of education." In discussing Dewey's educational ideas, keep in mind that education was not peripheral to his overall perspective, but as Richard Bernstein suggests, "the whole of philosophy."[53] Much like Matthew Lipman (Lipman's Philosophy for Children program is discussed in depth in the next chapter), Bernstein compares Dewey's educational ideas to the practice of Socrates. In the early dialogues of Plato, Socrates introduces the youth of Athens to "the subtleties of careful analysis."[54] Beginning with topics or objects of interest to his young companions, Socrates guides them to a discussion of increasingly complex and abstract issues such as the nature of friendship, fairness, and justice. In short, Socrates engages his young Athenians in the very Deweyian goal of critical thinking.

Socrates and Dewey share a common goal, that is, fostering intelligence in the young by introducing them to a community of inquiry in action. To Socrates and Dewey, intelligence meant more than drawing inferences and conclusions from explicit premises. To them, intelligence connotes habits of mind, that is, "the abilities to discern the complexities of situations; imagination that is exercised in seeing new possibilities and hypotheses; willingness to learn from experience; fairness and objectivity in judging and evaluating conflicting values and opinions; and the courage to change one's views when it is demanded by the consequences of our actions."[55] In short, Dewey and Socrates are alike in advocating as the ultimate educational goal the kind of wisdom Dewey associates with philosophy.

Fostering this kind of wisdom or intelligence is or should be the goal of all education. In 1916, Dewey suggested that by transforming schools into embryonic democracies, the school could be society's "chief agency for accomplishment of this end."[56] Later in his life he backed away from this optimistic and rather naive view of the power of schooling. Writing in 1937, Dewey states:

> It is unrealistic, in my opinion, to suppose that the schools can be a main agency in producing the intellectual and moral changes, the changes in attitudes and disposition of thought and purpose, which are necessary for the creation of a new social order. Any such view ignores the constant operation of powerful forces outside the school which shape mind and character. It ignores the fact that school education is but one educational agency out of many, and at the best is in some respects a minor educational force.[57]

It had become obvious to him that the teacher could not usher in "the true kingdom of God," but Dewey remained committed to democratic principles and to the importance of education, if not schooling, in fostering them. Realizing that transforming schools into embryonic democracies was not enough, Dewey remained steadfast in his commitment to democracy and to the kind of philosophical and educational wisdom necessary for creating this Great Community.

Dewey sees the philosopher playing a crucial role in the development of a democratic public. Philosophers can and should contribute to the conversation by presenting their investigations and insights regarding the dynamics of human associations in such a manner so as to enhance every individual's ability to contribute to the regulation of the community to which they find themselves in and/or choose to belong. The true value of these investigations is determined by how well they actually foster the kind of human associations that release individual potential and enrich the personal experiences of members of the community. By creatively addressing the problem of method, the philosopher contributes to development of an engaged citizenry comprised of wise amateurs committed to strong democratic institutions. By focusing on the art of presentation, the philosopher can play a significant role in enabling Dewey's vision of the Great Community to be realized.

RICHARD RORTY: YOU ARE NO JOHN DEWEY

In the previous chapter—and to a lesser degree in this one—the ideas of Richard Rorty and other postmodernists have been compared to those of John Dewey. It was suggested earlier that Rorty and other postmodernists are guilty of what Dewey referred to as either/or thinking. Using Kafka's parable to characterize the philosopher's dilemma of being caught in the middle between the warring forces of the past and the future, Rorty and other postmodernists concentrate on destroying or "deconstructing" the past. Dewey, on the other hand—his own attempts at overcoming tradition and at "closing down the epistemology industry"[58] well known—was not content with debunking the past. Rather than being content with philosophy as a parasite feeding upon or reacting to some historical field of thought, Dewey seeks to understand the past, not to preserve or sustain it, but to use it in forming a vision—albeit a temporal and contingent one—of what the future could and should be.

While Dewey joins forces with Rorty in urging philosophers to abandon foundational claims to knowledge, philosophy has more than just an edifying role to play. Fearing that "philosophy that was merely edifying would degenerate into little more than an expression of 'cloudy desire,'"[59] Dewey encourages philosophers to focus on the "problems of men" in order to help humankind in building a better future. Focusing on the "problems of men" meant understanding and even attacking the past as part of a larger effort of developing a positive vision of what could and should be. As previously noted, philosophy for Rorty is little more than playful, therapeutic criticism, at best helpful in debunking the false claims and institutions of the past but incapable of developing and sustaining an inspirational vision of what ought to be. Philosophy, when conceptualized as "an *intellectualized* wish" is, suggests Dewey, hard work, but work that is capable of producing such visions, however temporal and contingent, of what could and should be. These subtle, yet significant differences on the nature and role of philosophy makes it clear that Richard Rorty is no John Dewey.

In Conclusion: A Word of Caution

A major focus of this work is to try to understand the origins of educational philosophy, the current status of the field, and what the discipline ought to become. It is in pursuit of such understanding that Dewey's *Experience and Education* was discussed early in this chapter. Not only does this little volume introduce the themes that are crucial to the discussion offered in this chapter, that is, either/or thinking, but in this little work, Dewey offers an accessible, concise statement of his overall philosophy. In addition, a careful reading of *Experience and Education* produces insights into where and what educational philosophy ought to be. Dewey suggests "that those who are looking ahead to a new movement in education, adapted to the existing need for a new social order, should think in terms of Education itself rather than in terms of some 'isms' about education, even such 'ism' as progressivism."[60] In short, Dewey is suggesting that educational philosophy should look to education itself, rather than to the academic field of philosophy, to determine its future. Implicit in Dewey's admonition is his belief that in the connection between education and philosophy lies the origins of philosophy itself. As discussed previously, the relationship between education and philosophy is, at the very least, an intimate one. In the strongest sense, philosophy and education become one since all good philosophy is educational and all good education is philosophical.

This intimate union of philosophy is what is meant by philosophy *as* education. As a whole, this chapter, indeed this entire work, advocates this Deweyian view of educational philosophy, but a word of caution is needed here. We must not assume that Dewey's vision of the union of philosophy and education constitutes *the* philosophy of education. To reify Dewey's vision, to become a disciple of Dewey or follower of any other ideology is to abandon the philosophic quest. Dewey's vision provides us with a set of guidelines for reconstructing our field, but there is no one correct path or no one correct way of reconstructing educational philosophy. Philosophy *as* education can and should take many forms, or to use Dewey's terms, "different philosophies will exist, because men have in mind different ideals of life and different educational methods for making these ideas prevail."[61] To further illustrate this same point, Dewey noted more than sixty years ago that women's perspective is not and cannot be the same as that expressed by males. Even if women embrace Dewey's vision, they have experienced the world differently than men and as a result their concept of philosophy *as* education will be different.

While the characteristics of good or educative philosophy are identified and discussed earlier, these serve, at best, as guiding principles for our collective struggle to define what educational philosophy can and should be. In pursuit of possible directions for the field of educational philosophy to take, we turn now to a discussion of Matthew Lipman's attempts to turn philosophy inside out. Lipman's Philosophy for Children program exemplifies much of Dewey's thought, but a word of caution is needed here as well. Just as we must guard against reifying Dewey's thought, we should approach Lipman's claim that Philosophy for Children "is the only valid representative of Dewey's education theory put into practice" with skepticism.

Philosophy for Children: Implementing Dewey's Vision

Matthew Lipman is often asked how he came to write *Harry Stottlemeier's Discovery*. Since *Harry* was Lipman's first effort at developing what has become the internationally acclaimed Philosophy for Children program, the question usually means how did Lipman come to develop this innovative approach to dramatizing philosophy, or when and how did Lipman begin to sense that the erudite and highly professionalized field of philosophy could and should be made accessible to a larger audience, including children and youth? While this essay will discuss a few of the various explanations Lipman has offered regarding the origins of *Harry Stottlemeier's Discovery*, the central theme concerns Lipman's conceptualization of philosophy and his dramatization of it. Before we tackle these more complex questions, for those unfamiliar with what is meant by Philosophy for Children, a brief response to the question: "Who is Harry Stottlemeier and What Did He Discover?" is in order.

WHO IS HARRY STOTTLEMEIER?

Harry Stottlemeier is a fictitious fifth-grader whose mind wanders one day in Mr. Bradley's science class. After listening to Mr. Bradley explain the intricacies of the solar system, Harry begins to "picture in his mind the great, flaming sun, and all the little planets spinning steadily around it."[1] Suddenly the teacher asks him a question: "What is it that has a long tail, and revolves about the sun once every 77 years?" Not knowing the answer, Harry tries to figure out an answer. Knowing that all planets revolve about the sun, Harry reasons that this thing with a tail that revolves around the sun must be a planet.

His response is greeted with laughter, since everyone else had heard Mr. Bradley say that comets (in this case Halley's comet) revolve around the sun just as planets do but are definitely not planets. Embarrassed by the reactions of his classmates and upset for failing to answer the question, Harry wonders what went wrong. Thinking about what happened, Harry realizes that he erred in assuming that since all planets revolve around the sun, all things that revolve around the sun are planets.

Excited about this new discovery that "all" sentences can't be reversed, Harry hastens to tell Lisa about it. Lisa is one of his classmates, but Harry intuitively knew that she was not among those who laughed at him. With Lisa's help further discoveries are made, including a revision of his initial discovery. Together Harry and Lisa conclude that if a true sentence begins with the word *no*, then its reverse is also true; but if it begins with the word *all*, then its reverse is false.

Elated over his and Lisa's discoveries, Harry runs home to find his mother and a neighbor, Mrs. Olson, engaged in the following conversation:

> Mrs. Olson was saying, "Let me tell you something, Mrs. Stottlemeier. That Mrs. Bates, who just joined the PTA, every day I see her go into the liquor store. Now, you know how concerned I am about those unfortunate people who just can't stop drinking. Every day, I see them go into the liquor store. Well, that makes me wonder whether Mrs. Bates is, you know..."
>
> "Whether Mrs. Bates is like them?" Harry's mother asked politely.
>
> Mrs. Olson nodded. Suddenly something in Harry's mind went "CLICK!"
>
> "Mrs. Olson," he said, "just because, according to you, *all people who can't stop drinking* are *people who go to the liquor store*, that doesn't mean that *all people who go to the liquor store* are *people who can't stop drinking.*"
>
> "Harry," said his mother, "this is none of your business, and besides, you're interrupting."
>
> But Harry could tell by the expression on his mother's face that she was pleased with what he'd said. So he quietly got his glass of milk and sat down to drink it, feeling happier than he had felt in days.[2]

Though Lipman's ideas about dramatizing philosophy have evolved in the almost quarter of a century since he wrote this first chapter of *Harry*, one can still find in this episode the essential ideas found in all of the Philosophy for Children materials. Lipman has improved in his struggle to master the craft of dramatizing philosophy and his more recent efforts are much more sophisticated than *Harry Stottlemeier's Discovery*. Still, Harry's persistent struggle to figure things out—in Bruner's language, to go beyond the information given—is a thread that permeates all of the Philosophy for Children materials. Caught in the act of daydreaming, Harry unsuccessfully attempts to reason his way out of a predicament. Experiencing embarrassment as a result of his failure, he turns his reasoning inward and tries to figure out his mistake. Through such reflection, along with a little help from his friends, he begins to unravel the mysteries of thought and subsequently to apply his discoveries to his everyday world. In this brief, introductory episode, Lipman offers fifth and sixth graders a practical, and largely Deweyian model of how humans think. To the degree that students in the classroom identify with Harry and his friends, these students are likely to emulate them as they discover and apply the rules of reason. As a literary work, *Harry* is contrived and overly simplistic, but as a vehicle for enabling children and youth to participate in the philosophical enterprise, it remains as effective as Lipman's more recent and sophisticated works.

Including *Harry*, there are seven Philosophy for Children novels and accompanying instructional materials. *Harry* is largely used in fifth and sixth grade classrooms with *Lisa*, *Suki*, and *Mark* functioning as sequels and focusing on ethical, aesthetic, and social reasoning respectively. Lipman's more recent pedagogical novels—*Pixie*, *Kio and Gus*, and *Elfie*—are for elementary grade children and concentrate on language. The elementary, middle, and high school students using these materials grapple with the multiplicity of skills that characterize the philosopher's craft, but Philosophy for Children is as much art as craft. As Ronald F. Reed and Ann E. Richter explain

..., *Harry Stottlemeier's Discovery*, can be read as a cautionary tale in which children learn a few rules of reasoning—categorical syllogisms, hypothetical deductive syllogisms—and discover, to their frequent chagrin, that thinking has aesthetic and practical components that ought not be reduced to those rules. *Suki*—while dealing extensively with the mechanics of writing, especially in the manual that accompanies the novel—recognizes that the writing of poetry goes beyond that of a craft. *Mark* and *Lisa* place significant emphasis on empathy as an element in political and ethical reasoning. It is perhaps in the work geared toward younger children—*Elfie, Kio and Gus*, and most notably *Pixie*—that one sees most clearly how important an understanding of thinking that goes beyond that of simple skills development is for Philosophy for Children. For example, at the very heart of *Pixie* is what is arguably the most aesthetic of all reasoning, i.e. analogical reasoning.[3]

In each of the novels the main characters experience feelings of inadequacy or frustration. For example, Harry is concerned over thinking poorly while Lisa agonizes over the inconsistency between her thoughts and feelings. Suki is alarmed over Harry's inability to write, and Mark rebels against the legal authorities. Pixie is confused about mind-body relationships and Kio and Gus confront Gus's blindness. Elfie, the protagonist in the most recent of the Philosophy for Children novels, has difficulty in asking questions. These difficulties appear early in the narratives, with much of the remainder of each novel devoted to the children's attempts to come to grips with their problems. Each program emphasizes a particular aspect of the philosophical enterprise, but they all employ dialogue as an essential teaching strategy and have as their common goal the transformation of the classroom into a community of inquiry. Since dialogue and the community of inquiry play key roles in Lipman's attempts to turn philosophy inside out, the meaning and use of these ingredients are discussed in detail below.

FOSTERING A COMMUNITY OF INQUIRY THROUGH DIALOGUE[4]

Common to all the Philosophy for Children materials is the transformation of the elementary, middle, or high school classroom into a self-corrective community of inquiry. Key to such a transformation is the appropriate use of dialogue as a teaching strategy. Since, as already noted, the dialectical and pedagogical aspects of philosophy have similar roots, it is not surprising that the dialogical tradition can be traced back to ancient Greece of the sixth century B.C. It was at this time that the field of philosophy emerged, with literary forms serving as vehicles for presenting philosophical material. Whether in the aphorisms of Heraclitus, the poetry of Parmenides, or the dialogues of Plato, the literature of ancient times often contained philosophical material. By introducing it in this fashion, philosophical inquiry became more than just an academic or professional enterprise. Embodied in literary forms, philosophical inquiry was accessible to all educated persons.

Socrates, as portrayed in the dialogues of Plato, provides us with an excellent model of how discovery and understanding are enhanced through dialogue. Often conversing with the youth of Athens, Socrates models a process of intellectual inquiry that is rigorous but never condescending. Rather than imposing his own ideas and beliefs upon the impressionable young minds, Socrates demonstrates that thinking is hard work that no one can or should do for someone else. He models for his friends the difference between thinking and thinking well, and his enthusiasm for learning is contagious. Perhaps most significant is his ability to instill in these young men the confidence that they too can master the art of thinking well.

Socrates demands that his charges think, but more importantly he shows them how to think. He demonstrates that dialogue compels us to be on our toes intellectually. In such an activity there is no place for mindless banter or slovenly reasoning. When engaged in a serious conversation, listening is thinking because one needs to understand before one can evaluate other points of view. Speaking is thinking for one must weigh carefully each word to ensure that it conveys the meaning that is desired. To engage in dialogue is to rehearse in our minds what others have said, to assess the relevance and significance of these remarks, to recognize other perspectives than our own, and to explore possibilities that heretofore were unknown to us. As Socrates demonstrates, genuine dialogue avoids indoctrination by holding all points of view, including one's own, to the same rigorous examination. Thinking, everyone's thinking, is subjected to the most rigorous test of logic and experience. To do this is not easy but, as Socrates demonstrates, the establishment of a community of inquiry enhances the cooperative search for greater understanding.

While Plato's dialogues are still appropriate for today's young adults, little philosophical discourse is presented in dramatic form. In recent years philosophical discourse has become more technical and scientific, hence of interest only to the specialist, the academic philosopher. Yet what the Greeks discovered and Socrates modeled more than 2,000 years ago—that the unexamined life is not worth living—is as true today as it was then. Only by becoming reflective beings can humans gain understanding and meaning in this world. As Socrates demonstrates in Plato's dramatic dialogues, interaction among participants in a community of inquiry stimulates such self-reflection.

In order to transform classrooms into self-corrective communities of inquiry, children need a Socratic model to emulate. They need to read and talk about their peers, children like themselves struggling to figure things out. The Philosophy for Children novels help meet that need. Just as Socrates modeled a process of inquiry for the youth of Athens, and just as Plato's dialogues offer such a model for adults, the characters in the novels provide elementary, middle, and high school students with appropriate models of good thinking. Lipman, as the primary author of these works, has improved as a literary craftsman, but none of the novels qualify as great literature. They are intended as pedagogical novels, designed to offer children and youth a substantive intellectual diet around which to build a sturdy and lasting community of inquiry.

The philosophical ideas introduced in the novels serve as springboards for discussions of things that matter most to students. In such a community the discussion is more than just a question-and-answer session between the teacher and individual students. Ideally the conversation should be passed from student to student with the teacher participating as one of the group. In such a community all are committed, including the teacher, to follow reason wherever it leads. In order for such a community to develop, students must be encouraged to volunteer pertinent personal experiences or to offer different interpretations or perspectives. Discussions should initially focus on ideas or events in the novel of interest to students and progress to other ideas and interests suggested by the novel. Over time, as the community develops, students learn to value their own thoughts as well as the thoughts of others and to subject all ideas, including their own, to careful scrutiny.

Just as Socrates personified the examined life, the characters in the novels personify a community of inquiry in action. These characters demonstrate the characteristics of good intellectual inquiry, including efforts to figure things out, to go beyond the information given. In the novels, intellectual inquiry almost always occurs in a public place with two or more children and/or adults engaged in a conversation about something that is puzzling to them. Like Harry's daydreaming episode at the beginning of this chapter, discussion in the novels is usually initiated by one of the children upon encountering a confusing situation. The conversation begins as the character seeks help from friends in trying to figure out a solution. While the problem is usually philosophical in nature, of more significance is the children's manner of coping with it. Naively sharing their sense of wonder, these children demonstrate a willingness to express their most private thoughts; to admit to their own ignorance or bewilderment; to overcome their fears of being different, foolish, or stupid. The characters in the novels take risks, modeling their collective belief that progress in solving problems is possible. While progress is made, the quest never ends. As the solution to one's puzzle is discovered or invented, additional problems emerge in the mind of another. As the inquiry continues, the characters become actors in a kind of never-ending story.

In addition to demonstrating the positive results that a community of inquiry can produce, characters in the novels model different styles of thinking in their collective struggle to figure things out. Students in the classroom quickly note that certain characters are risk-takers, while others are more cautious; some are analytical, while others are experimental; and some are empirical, while others are speculative. Students readily grasp that there is no one right way of thinking and that progress is best achieved when individuals possessing different styles of thinking focus on common problems.

Provided with numerous examples of a heterogeneous community of inquiry in action, students in the classroom tend to identify with and emulate characters in the novels. As students in the classroom seriously consider the ideas introduced in or generated by the novels, they are compelled to reflect, to concentrate, to listen closely to others, to assess and evaluate ways of examining an issue that previously never occurred to them. Through this process the classroom is transformed into a community of inquiry. Participants, perhaps unknowingly at first, begin to develop and hone what are currently known as higher order thinking skills. While specific acts and skills needed to succeed in such higher order thinking can be identified, thinking well involves the selection, coordination, and application of specific skills in response to a particular problem. In a sense it is not possible to teach this, since thinking well means thinking for oneself—an activity that no one can or should do for us. But an atmosphere to encourage the recognition, selection, and application of appropriate thinking skills can be created. As Socrates demonstrated, genuine dialogue assumes a method of inquiry where all ideas and thoughts are scrutinized in the search for greater understanding. As part of his efforts to revive this Socratic ideal, Matthew Lipman developed the Philosophy for Children materials for the purpose of converting classrooms into communities of inquiry.

In developing the Philosophy for Children program, Lipman focused his energies on what he calls the rational curriculum. Still, in pursuit of his goal of transforming philosophy into the foundational discipline for children and youth, Lipman could not ignore the importance of training teachers to convert their classrooms into communities of inquiry. Guiding a philosophical discussion is an art that few teachers have mastered. It requires an understanding of when and when not to intervene in the discussion. It requires skill in eliciting views and opinions from students and in helping them to discover the logical implications of their views. Orchestrating a philosophical discussion means attending to thoughts and points of view volunteered by students, weaving the threads together, and assisting students to understand that their ideas make a difference in their lives. Like Socrates, a teacher of philosophical inquiry must be a gadfly, admonishing students to be intellectual risk-takers, encouraging them to think for themselves, aiding them in the search for more comprehensive solutions.

Teachers committed to philosophical inquiry can, with practice, develop the skill needed to conduct a philosophical dialogue. But first, they must have retained some of their childlike wonder. They must be intellectually open and honest, curious about as well as critical of the world, knowledgeable but not all-knowing. In addition, they need coaching in the art of conducting philosophical inquiry. Teachers who are genuinely committed to philosophical inquiry (not all are) and who respect the opinions of children can, with training, successfully implement the Philosophy for Children program. In devising numerous strategies for preparing teachers to use these materials in their classrooms, Lipman and his associates all agree that teachers must understand and experience the power of a community of inquiry if they expect to convert their classroom into one.

MATTHEW LIPMAN: THE ACADEMIC

While others have contributed to making Philosophy for Children an internationally acclaimed thinking skills program, it is Matthew Lipman's genius that created these materials and that sustains this effort at turning philosophy inside out. In an attempt to better understand Lipman and his view of the nature of philosophy, a brief biographical sketch is offered, followed by a more critical exposition of the origins of Philosophy for Children.

A native of New Jersey, Matthew Lipman graduated high school in 1940. His undergraduate experience, which included study at Stanford University, Shrivenham American University in England, and Columbia University, was accompanied by three years of military service during World War II. Receiving his B.S. in General Studies from Columbia in 1948, Lipman continued at Columbia University for graduate work where, as well as at the Sorbonne in Paris and at the University of Vienna, he studied philosophy for six more years. Receiving his doctorate from Columbia in 1954, Lipman embarked on an academic career, holding a variety of teaching and administrative positions over the next twenty years.

During this period, Lipman was affiliated in various ways with Brooklyn College, Mannes College of Music, Sarah Lawrence College, the Baruch School of City College of New York, and, of course, Columbia University, where he served as chair of the Department of General Education, College of Pharmaceutical Sciences from 1962 to 1972.

During this period, Lipman's scholarly interests focused largely on aesthetics. In addition to two books—*What Happens in Art* and *Contemporary Aesthetics*—Lipman achieved recognition for reviews of Ernest Mundt's *Art, Form, and Civilization*; Milton C. Nalm's *The Artist as Creator*; and Nelson Goodman's *Languages of Art in Man and World*; and for his articles "The Relations of Critical Functions and Critical Decisions to Art Inquiry," "The Physical Thing in Aesthetic Experience," and "The Aesthetic Presence of the Body." In addition, Lipman published a moderately successful introductory philosophy text.

As will be discussed below, Philosophy for Children began in 1969, but it was not until Lipman became affiliated with Montclair State College in Upper Montclair, New Jersey that the program began to take shape. Here, along with Ann Margaret Sharp, Lipman established the Institute for the Advancement for the Philosophy for Children and embarked on what has become his life's work of restoring the connection between philosophy and education by turning philosophy inside out. In these past twenty-plus years, Lipman's productivity has been remarkable, producing a high volume of significant works that genuinely reconnects philosophy and education. In addition to the seven Philosophy for Children novels and accompanying instructional manuals, Lipman is the single or lead author of *Philosophy in the Classroom*; *Growing Up With Philosophy*; *Philosophy Goes to School*; and *Thinking in Education*. In addition, Lipman has published more than 60 articles and had his works translated into the German, French, Egyptian, Hebrew, Chinese, Danish, Spanish, Italian, and Icelandic languages. He has also edited *Thinking: The Journal of Philosophy for Children*, conducted over a hundred Philosophy for Children workshops for professors of philosophy and teachers, and given more than two hundred presentations to a variety of audiences throughout the world.[5]

THE ORIGINS OF PHILOSOPHY FOR CHILDREN

To use the vernacular, it has been quite a ride, but where and how did it all begin? As noted in the introductory paragraph, Lipman has been asked, over and over again, how this strange adventure got started.

Lipman reports that he answers truthfully but differently each time he is asked this question. According to Professor Lipman, "there are histories, but no History, and if I were to live as long as Methuselah, these histories would continue to become still more numerous and more divergent."[6] Lipman is reluctant to offer such autobiographical accounts, fearing that they will obscure rather than illuminate the development of Philosophy for Children. Lipman suggests that any portrayal of a lived life and its accomplishments, including a self-portrait, is at best a partial reconstruction of the events that contributed to the direction one took or the product produced. Any biography or autobiography traces connections, but both the author and the audience need to understand that the connections presented are as much inventions as discoveries.

With this word of caution, Lipman has in recent years been a bit more forthcoming in discussing how and when Philosophy for Children came to be. In a work in process, Lipman provides us with snippets or glimpses of the seminal experiences and individuals that contributed to his embracing turning philosophy inside out as his mission in life. One such individual was his cousin and her husband, Evelyn and Joseph Isaacson. Characterizing them as his parental equivalents, Lipman suggests that he got to know them when he was about fifteen years old. Joe's interest in the arts particularly impressed young Matthew, as did Mr. Isaacson's "probing, critical, but never unfriendly intelligence." Lipman adds "Without that momentary encounter, I might not have welcomed philosophy as warmly as I did when I learned about it four years later, at Stanford. His ready sympathy with all disinterested inquiry has provided me ever since with a living criterion of intellectual inquiry."[7] Lipman credits the Isaacsons with, many years later, introducing him to the art of children and their education. During the sixties as he visited with them at their home in Pound Ridge, New York, Lipman suggests that "our conversations would turn more and more frequently to the topic of education."[8] Though Lipman does not go so far as to suggest that the idea for *Harry* came directly from the Isaacsons, he did, he tells us, discuss the possibility of such a work with them in 1968.

Lipman acknowledges his indebtedness to John Dewey, suggesting that Philosophy for Children "is the only valid representative of Dewey's educational theory put into practice,"[9] but where and how did Lipman encounter Dewey's thought. Lipman tells us his exposure occurred while in the Army during World War II participating in a special program at Stanford University. Here Carl Thomas introduced him to philosophy in general and to John Dewey indirectly. From Professor Thomas, young Mat Lipman learned the importance of grounding "one's theories in *concreta*."[10] As he was leaving Stanford to rejoin his infantry unit, Thomas gave Lipman a paperback book called *Philosopher's Holiday* by Irwin Edman. Edman was a member of the Philosophy Department at Columbia University, and his book was largely about "his recollections of Dewey."[11] Lipman was intrigued by both Dewey and Columbia, resolving to go there once the war was over. Purchasing a copy of Dewey's *Intelligence in the Modern World*, Lipman understood little of it but carried it in his duffel bag as his division traversed Europe, eventually joining Patton's Third Army in Germany and ending up in Austria. Lipman tells us that for many years what he knew of Dewey's educational ideas were derived as inferences from this work.

The influence of Dewey notwithstanding, there were other, non-American influences to the birthing of Philosophy for Children. At midcentury, Lipman returned to Paris to study at the Sorbonne. Spending eighteen months there on a Fulbright scholarship, Lipman discovered, through his study of Diderot and others, that it was "possible to discuss profound philosophical ideas with ease and clarity." Resonating to Diderot's and other encyclopediasts' attempts to "establish a *rapprochement* between the expert and the man in the street, between theory and practice, and between art and craft," Lipman acknowledges that "Diderot did much to shape my convictions about the role of philosophy in the public sphere."[12] In Paris, Lipman also encountered and read an article in the French periodical *Deucalion* written by the German exile Bernhard Groethuysen titled "The Child and the Metaphysician." Using the life of Kierkegaard to illustrate, the article demonstrated "how intimately the thinking of children and the thinking of philosophers resembled each other."[13] These French seeds were planted in the mind of a young Matthew Lipman awaiting the right circumstances to germinate and bear fruit.

Upon returning to the States and completing his Ph.D. at Columbia, Lipman settled into a promising, if somewhat ordinary academic career. His confidence in the healing powers of philosophy was shaken but not destroyed by the disturbances at Columbia University during the late sixties. Concerned that neither students nor faculty, including philosophers, exhibited good judgment during the riots of 1968, Lipman took solace "in the process of *doing* philosophy rather than in the supposed wisdom of any products resulting from that process."[14] Since neither the faculty nor the students were reasoning very well, Lipman began to question the efficacy of teaching logic to undergraduates.

Gradually he concluded that both his students and his peers had been miseducated and that no amount of philosophy or logic could remedy the situation at this late hour. It was too late to help the current generation of undergraduates, but philosophy as conceptualized by

Socrates, by Frenchmen like Diderot, and by Dewey might still save future generations.

In a sense, the disturbances of the late sixties proved to be fortuitous for Lipman for they enabled him to identify his mission in life. Though he expressed it differently then, and had yet to develop the skill to operationalize his vision, Lipman consciously set out to turn philosophy inside out and to restore its natural connection to education. Lipman's strategy for accomplishing this ambitious task "was to change the supply of students coming into the university,"[15] thus eventually forcing a change in the faculty. Harking back to the similarities between a child's thinking and that of a philosopher, the key was to keep alive the natural inquisitiveness and sense of wonder that children bring with them to kindergarten.

At about this time, Rita Nadler, a lawyer and neighbor whose children attended the same schools as Lipman's, shared with him her impressions of the school. During this conversation, Lipman suggested that "schools ought to offer a course in reasoning, similar to what (he) was teaching ... at CCNY and Columbia."[16] She responded enthusiastically to the idea, adding "you could make it in the form of a story..." Although he was initially skeptical, the idea kept him awake at night, and when combined with the ongoing conversations with the Isaacsons as well as numerous other factors, culminated in the creation of *Harry Stottlemeier's Discovery*.

Once the issue of introducing children to the philosophical enterprise by means of a story was broached, the question became: what kind of a story? Using narrative to convey philosophical ideas was not new, but writing a children's version of Will Durant's *The Story of Philosophy* was not the answer. Lipman thought of stories that fascinated him as a child, and was convinced that the story must be for and about children. The story must be told from the child's point of view with the participants in the story constituting "a small community of inquiry, in which everyone shared, at least to some extent, in cooperatively searching for and discovering ways of thinking."[17]

Unlike regular novels, the plot was purposefully thin and there was little character development. The children were distinguished from one another more by their style of thinking than by character traits. Lipman explains, "one could be experimental, another intuitive, a third analytical, a fourth skeptical and so on, although no one style would be presented as inherently better or worse than any other."[18] The story line, as described in the introductory pages of this essay, developed around the process of inquiry with the children discovering and applying the principle of logical conversion. Throughout *Harry* and other Philosophy for Children novels, a skeleton plot is used merely as a vehicle for engaging students in the classroom and introducing them to the ideas and skills that comprise the philosophical tradition. Though Lipman may have dreamed of *Tom Sawyer*, he settled for much less. Certainly the first Philosophy for Children novel is not great, or even good literature, but as a text designed to introduce fifth and sixth graders to the philosophical enterprise, it has few equals.

Arriving at a title for the novel also presented problems. Seeking to follow Plato's example of naming the dialogue after the chief protagonist, and since Lipman planned to begin the novel with "a bit of Aristotle's logic," he began looking for a name that resembled Aristotle. After several failures, Lipman came across Mel Stottlemeyr, a rookie pitcher for the New York Yankees and that was all he needed. The chief protagonist became Harry Stottlemeier, a patient, exploratory, eleven year old "given to alternating moods of wonder and self-doubt."[19] As a young contemporary Aristotle, Harry and friends introduced students in the classroom to the rules of reason by modeling a community of inquiry in action.

WHY PHILOSOPHY?

Matthew Lipman joins Rorty, Dewey, and others in criticizing the social impotence of professional philosophy, but Lipman takes this critique a step further. Perhaps Lipman is guilty of hyperbole when he suggests that Philosophy for Children is the only extant educational program that effectively implements Dewey's educational ideas. Still, in struggling to remake philosophy so as to make it accessible to all, Lipman has been guided by the Deweyan belief that the habits that a genuine democracy requires can be developed. In developing philosophical novels for and about children and youth, Lipman implemented the Deweyan principles that "presentation is fundamentally important" and that democracy begins in "the neighborly community." The result is a program that combines the dialectical and pedagogical aspects of philosophy.

Lipman acknowledges his indebtedness to Dewey, but, as previously discussed, it is in Socrates that he finds the personification of the role philosophy should play in our lives. According to Lipman, "What Socrates models for us is not philosophy known or philosophy applied but philosophy practiced. He (Socrates) challenges us to acknowledge that philosophy as deed, as form of life, is something that any of us could emulate."[20]

As previously noted, philosophy first appeared about a hundred generations ago, "embodied in aphorisms, poetry, dialogue, and drama."[21] For reasons already noted, these educative, philosophical vehicles have largely disappeared, and with them philosophy's public role.

This kind of philosophy, this Socratic version of it, must be revived if Dewey's vision is ever to be realized. To achieve this end we must recognize that the doing of philosophy is emblematic of shared inquiry as a way of life and that "one does not have to be a philosopher to foster the self corrective spirit of inquiry, rather it can and should be fostered in each and every one of our institutions."[22]

While philosophy as characterized above should pervade all our institutions, it frequently does not. This is all the more reason why our schools should embody and foster this Socratic view of philosophy. While this ideal is far from being achieved, Lipman's "Philosophy for Children" program has succeeded in making the philosophical tradition accessible to children and youth. By exposing students to issues and ideas that are important and problematic to them, students gradually learn to create and control a community to which they belong. Like Dewey's embryonic democracies, these self-reflective communities of inquiry may have a ripple effect, contributing to the creation of larger and larger democratic communities.

As discussed earlier, a major, if not the primary goal of Philosophy for Children is to convert elementary, middle, and secondary school classrooms into communities of inquiry. The term "community of inquiry" is usually associated with the pragmatists, most notably Pierce and Dewey, but as we have seen, the idea goes back much further. Lipman suggests that it can be found in ancient Athens exemplified in the teachings of Socrates. But creating a community of inquiry requires more than mastery of the Socratic method. While Lipman recognizes that a knowledgeable teacher or other adult is important in helping children and youth to create and participate in a community of inquiry, Lipman considers the text or content to be a more crucial element. Put succinctly, Lipman believes that content does matter and, more importantly, the content of philosophy is the preferred subject matter.

Lipman characterizes philosophy as a unique discipline, a content that is both "abstract and meaningful."[23] It consists of a "core of concepts" to be "analyzed, discussed, interpreted, and clarified."[24] While we often experience these concepts in the particular, we do not truly understand them until we can appreciate them in the abstract. Lipman explains by suggesting that "everything concrete has an abstract envelope. We can experience things themselves, but we can understand them only by getting to know the envelopes that enclose them."[25] Philosophy, suggests Lipman, seeks to find or create that abstract or universal envelope to frame or define a concrete, particular experience. By introducing children and youth to such core concepts as friendship, fairness, truth, or justice, the Philosophy for Children novels discourage students from resting "content with this or that particular instance or variety of truth," and pushes them to "consider if there is such a thing as truth in general, or 'the truth'."[26]

It is from this somewhat traditional view of philosophy that Lipman derives his position that a text, specifically a philosophical text, is of crucial importance in mediating between the culture and the child. Here Lipman parts company with many educational theorists, including Dewey, in suggesting that "the major burden of mediation should be borne by the text," not the teacher. Lipman suggests that his position is hardly unique, but merely a contemporary version of "the pedagogical role Plato expected his dialogues to play..."[27] By emulating Plato's dialogues, Lipman's pedagogical novels can serve "as a springboard for discussion, and discussion in turn is the matrix of student thinking."[28] Lipman admits that the Philosophy for Children materials cannot stand alone as philosophical material, but suggests they can generate genuine philosophical discourse among children and youth.

As noted earlier, not all texts contain the core philosophical concepts that are necessary for fostering philosophical discourse. Suggesting that fostering philosophical discussion is analogous to the refining of ores, Lipman explains that "low-grade ores need high-grade equipment" while "high-grade ores can be refined using only low-grade equipment."[29] Only experts are typically interested in discussing inanimate objects—"like paleontologists discussing rock strata," but it doesn't take much to interest children and other amateurs in a discussion of such philosophical concepts as justice, truth, and fairness. This explains why purposefully thin plots are appropriate for the Philosophy for Children novels for it only takes "a snippet of Heraclitus here, or Duns Scotus Erigina there, or Jean-Paul Sartre somewhere else"[30] to enable the reader to reconstruct the original argument. Clearly, from Lipman's perspective, the text, more so than the teacher, is the crucial element necessary for creating a community of inquiry.

Consistent with his goal of turning philosophy inside out is Lipman's criticism of curriculum developers. Such developers make curricula aimed "at the level where the children who will be using those curricula supposedly are—or at a level higher than the level at which those students are judged to be."[31] Lipman suggests that such curriculum development presupposes a stage theory of maturation that defines the intellectual capability of students at each phase of their development. Lipman proposes to replace such maturation curriculum development with a curriculum based on rationality.

Committed to the assumption that "students try to live up to (or down to) the level at which they are treated," Lipman favors "making curricula logical and rational in their sequencing rather than episodically and arbitrarily developmental."[32] Lipman suggests that "we ask ourselves which cognitive skills presuppose which and then endeavor to foster practice in the more primitive ones first so that these will be in place when the next group of skills is to be practiced."[33] For Lipman, one of the more primitive or basic of human reasoning skills is distinguishing between similarities and differences.

Distinction making is one of the very first skills focused on in the Philosophy for Children program. Attention to similarities and differences provides the focus for *Elfie*—designed for first and second grade children—and builds toward more sophisticated comparisons, including the distinctions between similes, metaphors, and analogies found in *Pixie*. Building upon these foci of the elementary Philosophy for Children curriculum is the treatment of one of the basic building blocks of formal logic introduced in the first chapter of *Harry Stottlemeier's Discovery* and summarized in the beginning paragraphs of this chapter. This, of course, is conversion, a special case of reversibility. Reversibility is a form of reciprocity and by providing students in the classroom with examples of kids like themselves engaged in social acts of reciprocity, transitivity, symmetry, and the like, Lipman explains that students begin to internalize the logic of relations. By recognizing particular and largely social instances of reciprocity, students are motivated to seek the logical kernel or "abstract understanding of reversibility."[34]

Lipman advocates and has attempted to construct such a rational curriculum. In a rational curriculum "each particular subject area should be more than just a heap of information to be doled out scoop by scoop, day after day. Each subject should unfold, build on itself, question itself, illuminate from within."[35] For this to succeed, two preconditions are required. First, the curriculum must be offered in the narrative rather than in expository form; and second, philosophy must assume its natural educational role as the foundational discipline for children and youth.

TURNING PHILOSOPHY INSIDE OUT

The impact that the ancients—especially Socrates, Plato, and Aristotle—have had on Lipman's thought has been referred to throughout this chapter. In many ways, Lipman's own beliefs reflect a classical philosophical position, but he does not follow the ancients' lead in placing philosophy at the pinnacle of the educational system. Rather than considering philosophy to be the capstone or culminating discipline in the educational hierarchy, Lipman suggests philosophy is best suited to serve as an introductory discipline for it prepares students to think in the other disciplines. From Lipman's perspective, philosophy is not the monarch of the disciplines, but it should be recognized for its ability to cultivate higher-order, complex thinking in every discipline.

Lipman argues that while each discipline may have its own distinct culture and content, their methodologies are more alike than different. Lipman contends that, "to a considerable extent, logic and scientific method are generic..."[36] From this perspective it follows that courses in generic methodology are needed for all students, and the earlier the better. A major component of philosophy is, for Lipman, this self-corrective method of inquiry. Add to this an equally important imaginative component and philosophy becomes the one discipline that spans the gulf between science and the arts.

Lipman has devoted the past third of his life to turning philosophy inside out. Perhaps he is guilty of special pleading when he suggests that philosophy should demonstrate for the other disciplines how to dramatize themselves. Such dramatization is necessary if philosophy is to do what Dewey suggests that it should do, that is, deal with the problems of humankind. In a similar vein, for the other disciplines to be understood and used by more than just the cultural and professional elite, they too need to be dramatized and operationalized. Unlike Rorty, who is content if philosophy can keep the conversation going, Lipman believes that philosophy is uniquely qualified to foster the development of an educated citizenry required in a democracy. In dramatizing philosophy—by making it accessible to a general public, including children and youth, Lipman has provided us with an important, albeit imperfect model for reconstructing educational philosophy. It is perhaps the ultimate irony that an individual who purportedly trusts neither philosophers nor educators has shown us how philosophy can make peace with education.

CONCLUSION: A WORD OF CAUTION

Lipman's Philosophy for Children program builds upon Dewey's ideas, but a word of caution is needed here. Those of us involved in Philosophy for Children need to be reminded that Lipman's approach is not the only, and may not be the best way of reviving Dewey's vision. While Lipman envisions philosophy as playing a more significant role than that of Rorty's edifying philosopher, some question whether Philosophy for Children is sufficiently radical to promote the kind of strong democracy that Dewey advocates. As noted in the previous chapter, Dewey had second thoughts about the efficacy of schooling, if not education, in fostering genuine democracy. Lipman articulates no such second thoughts and seems content with a weaker version of democracy than that advocated by Dewey. Whatever his reasoning, Lipman clearly retains his faith in the power of a properly designed rational curriculum, grounded in a properly constructed view of philosophy, to play a significant role in the creation and sustainment of a democratic social order.

To some, Philosophy for Children plays it safe. From this perspective, Lipman's program approximates what Henry Giroux and Michael Apple pejoratively refer to as a model curriculum. As such it succeeds in addressing one of the two broad categories upon which a curriculum should focus; namely "how the very texture of the day to day classroom relationships generates different meanings, restraints, cultural values, and social relationships;" but fails to illustrate "how schools function to reproduce, in both the hidden and formal curricula, the cultural beliefs and economic relationships that support the larger social order."[37] To the extent that Giroux and Apple's critiques of "model" curriculums fit Lipman's program, perhaps Philosophy for Children is better suited to preparing citizens for "thin," rather than strong democracies. From the perspective of Giroux and others, the time has come to move beyond both Dewey and Lipman to a more radical conception of pedagogy and democracy.

The criticism that Giroux's perspective suggests—that Philosophy for Children is too sanitized to effectively promote strong democracy— needs to be addressed if, as is suggested here, the field of educational philosophy is to benefit from the path blazed by Dewey and Lipman. Philosophy for Children embraces many of Dewey's ideas, but is it "the only valid representative of Dewey's educational theory put into practice?"

Lipman and those of us involved in Philosophy for Children should take pride in all that Philosophy for Children is and has accomplished, but we must not reify this approach or program as the one best program or approach to deal with the problems of humankind. There is no one correct way of reviving Dewey's vision, and no single approach (however brilliant) can put into practice Dewey's educational theory. Dewey's vision is not a product to be attained or a goal to be reached. Like his definition of philosophy itself, it is an "intellectualized wish" which by its very elusiveness enables humankind to remain forward-looking and optimistic. Any attempt to reify Dewey's vision denies that very same vision. Lipman's contribution to the redesign of philosophy so as to reconnect it to its educational origins is significant, but his is not the only voice calling for a revival of Dewey's vision. Our best hope of resurrecting Dewey is to entertain the multitude of voices trying to be heard. The field of educational philosophy in its struggle to define itself can learn much from Lipman's attempt to turn philosophy inside out, but other, heretofore excluded voices also need to be heard as the field charts its course for the future. These other voices will not lead us to certainty, but they contribute to our collective needs. As Jane Roland Martin suggests, these needs are "Acquaintanceship and conversation, not discipleship and dogma."[38]

The issue of discipleship is discussed in depth in the final chapter, but for now it is enough to suggest that this Deweyian vision of what philosophy should be—identified earlier as philosophy as education—means that philosophy can neither be known nor applied. It must be practiced. We can practice philosophy and empower others to do the same by engaging them in conversation on problematic issues of importance to them. Herein lies the link between philosophy and education, for the problematic generates thinking. Philosophy practiced is philosophy as education, and Philosophy for Children is one very significant example that the field of educational philosophy can and should emulate. Philosophy practiced, that is, philosophy as education, that is, what educational philosophy ought to be, contributes to the creation of a democratic society. Related and equally important for our purposes, philosophy practiced is rooted in the assumption that "all true philosophy is educational and all true education is philosophical."[39]

Educational Philosophy: Discipleship or Pilgrimage?

In a somewhat whimsical piece entitled "John Dewey's Disciples," William Van Til concludes:

> There's a great difference between the students of Dewey and the disciples of Dewey. Disciples turn Dewey's magnificent contribution into authoritarian dogma complete with writ, expounders and disputatious sects. They turn Dewey into a saint.... I suppose he's the first relativistic saint in all history.[1]

Apparently the occasion for such remarks was the "big doings in celebration of John Dewey's ninetieth birthday."[2] Assuming that the piece is autobiographical, Professor Van Til's spouse shares with him an account of the celebration offered in the morning newspaper. She says, "Here's an educator who says that Dewey is forever enshrined, for his writings are the fount of all educational knowledge. He goes on to say that Dewey has pronounced the ultimate word in world thought."[3]

"To think that it's happening to John Dewey too," responds Van Til. Like the many great thinkers that had preceded him, John Dewey was being canonized and those studying his thought were becoming his disciples. As the conversation over coffee continued, Van Til's wife asked "And what on earth is wrong with being a disciple of John Dewey?" Confronting her husband, she added that as one who had spent your life "putting John Dewey's ideas into practice in public schools," "you're a disciple of John Dewey yourself." While Van Til acknowledges that he is an admirer and a continuous student of the thought of John Dewey, he emphatically denies being a disciple of the great thinker. By way of explanation he suggests:

> By disciple I mean the person who treats Dewey's writings as though they were the final authority, the truth with a capital T, the eternal verity. A Dewey disciple—not a Dewey student or admirer, mind you—seems to regard Dewey's writings as a body of sacred writ. He quarrels with other disciples over the "true" meaning of the writ. To "prove" pet contentions, he cites something Dewey wrote near the turn of the nineteenth century. His opponent, in turn, proves the contrary by quoting something Dewey wrote forty years later. Each regards deviation from Dewey as the ultimate heresy—unless the master can be cited to justify the deviation....Unconsciously these disciples are authoritarian, not experimental. Regarding Dewey's great contribution as a gospel denies everything Dewey stands for! That is not what old John Dewey means at all![4]

This little narrative captures both the theme of this chapter and the purpose of this book as a whole. As suggested earlier, once the philosopher embraces a particular system or approach as the one correct perspective, that person ceases to be a philosopher. As we shall see, such abandonment of the spirit of inquiry means the denial of a philosophical spirit that is uniquely American. For philosophy—including educational philosophy—to flourish, it needs to reconceptualize itself as a pilgrimage that is never consummated, rather than the fountain of all knowledge from which only a few are allowed to drink. As explained in the following section, such a reconceptualization requires that philosophers abandon the almost natural inclination to assume the role of a disciple to a particular system or approach for the role of a pilgrim on a continuous, never-ending quest for greater understanding.

DISCIPLESHIP OR PILGRIMAGE?

In an article appearing in *Ed Theory* in 1955, Everett J. Kircher suggests that "American democracy has evolved to its present state without benefit of any single system of philosophy."[5] More recently, John E. Smith suggests that as Americans "perhaps we should not lament the absence of a recognizable `national' tradition in philosophy when we consider how restricting that can be, a block to the path of inquiry."[6] Kircher attributes whatever successes our democratic society has achieved to our nation's lack of a state ideology and compares our progress with that of the Soviet Union under doctrinaire and dogmatic Marxist-Leninism. Though writing in the 1950s, the events of recent months and years give his ideas added significance. Kircher argues that

> their (the Soviet Union) fatal error in judgement revealed itself in their uncompromising conviction that a distinguished system of thought could be made so logically adequate that it could be put into practice without fundamental modification.[7]

In words that seem even more meaningful thirty years later, Kircher adds

> It is therefore unfortunate that so many of us have been pre-occupied with the notion that the Russian error was in the selection of a wrong philosophy that we have neglected to note their more fundamental error; namely that they embrace the inhumanity of attempting to integrate their social order, and finally the world, in accordance with some one pre-planned and elaborately conceived philosophy.[8]

As Kircher notes, Americans have not been completely immune to such lunacy. Philosophers, including educational philosophers, particularly at times when the reforming zeal is popular or when the pressures for academic respectability are great, are especially susceptible to such tendencies.

This should surprise no one for at least one of the roles of the philosopher is to develop conceptual schemes that seemingly "knit the disparate...tag end of things into clear and consistent wholes..."[9] This quest for a unifying schema or theory is one of the defining characteristics of philosophy. Historically this has meant striving for the philosopher's stone, meaning either some all-encompassing truth or the correct path or method to the truth. Once attained, this truth would enable humankind to live in peace, prosperity, and harmony with one another. As Kircher explains "this is a noble dream which the over-agitated and the over-eager recurrently discover that they are destined to fulfill in reality." In short, those "who seek the philosopher's stone too expectantly find it. There is a compulsion in their quest which guarantees a premature discovery."[10] When one claims to have found the philosopher's stone—and many over the centuries have made that claim—one is in fact claiming to have discovered the "philosophy of philosophies." Using more modern language such a discovery might be referred to as *a* or *the* metanarrative. Whatever it is called once such a discovery is made—or more accurately when an individual or group of individuals think that such a discovery has been made—the philosophic quest ends and dogma, discipleship, and authoritarianism begins.

The problem lies not in the quest but in the reification of the products of the quest. As Kircher explains, the quest is natural, inevitable, and, in a sense proper. It is proper if the quest remains an unfinished aspiration. Paradoxically the philosopher's quest for the one unifying schema or theory must never be fulfilled if the philosophic spirit is to survive. The philosopher's quest is a pilgrimage that can never be consummated.

For this quest to remain healthy, philosophers

> need what they hasten to deny; they need an abundance of as yet unexplained problems, aspects of the natural world and of the human enterprises that have as yet been unable to assimilate into their organic structure. Moreover they need cross-fertilization with other systems of philosophy which they commonly attack with the intention of annihilation.[11]

While the quest for greater understanding of the human condition is a worthy and uniquely human phenomenon, Kircher warns us against "the all too human tendency to universalize this uniqueness and presume to assimilate all relevant diversity into one inclusive perspective..." denying humankind of its only real freedom in the process—"the freedom to engage life with integrity each on his own terms."[12] Comparing systems of philosophy to a cat in the forest, Kircher suggests that philosophies grow by what they feed upon and by transforming this feed into themselves. In their desire for some all-encompassing perspective or unifying schema, historically philosophers have assimilated or discarded other perspectives. While other, competing perspectives may be offered a special place in this larger system, Kircher suggests that "no matter how many birds a compassionate cat may eat, it never becomes birdlike...Regardless of high promises on the part of any system of thought to protect the distinctiveness of other organic forms within its own system,"[13] such distinctiveness is often lost as it is absorbed into or overwhelmed by the more dominate philosophic system.

Kircher's insights into the nature of philosophy seem particularly true of both the "implicative" and "applicative" views of educational philosophy. Since both are derivative of the parent discipline, those embracing a particular system or approach to educational philosophy run the risk of being victimized by the "ism" or approach they have adopted. To the extent that such `philosophers' reify the "ism" or approach to which they profess allegiance, they lose their ability to philosophize. Whether it is a Mortimer Adler promoting the educational implications of Aristotle or advocates of the analytic school suggesting that their approach has solved or will solve all philosophical problems, both are, however unwittingly, "calling for the abandonment of the philosophic enterprise."[14]

Philosophers who are so committed to a particular system or approach that they are uncompromising in their opposition to thought that conflicts with "their" own have become victims of the appropriated system or approach. They are not free to follow the philosophic quest wherever it may lead. They are bound by their discipleship to a particular person, system, or approach.

Contrast this to the philosopher as pilgrim. Such a philosopher finds "freedom in creating distinctive modes of thought out of the philosophic heritage and the occasion of its time. Former systems of thought are reconstructed rather than simply followed, implemented, and applied. Any philosopher worthy of the name is therefore the beneficiary of the philosophies of the past but never the victim of any one of them."[15]

An alternative suggests Kircher is to choose the "faith of the pilgrim rather than the disciple." This faith is characterized by "the commitment to the unending quest in which one's way is enlightened by all systems of thought but not fully directed by any one of them."[16] Kircher suggests that it is the rare individual who chooses the path of a pilgrim, but for those few who have chosen and do choose this path it leads "not to an ultimate dogma but to wisdom." With such wisdom comes a kind of humility for "in a state of wisdom (the pilgrim) discovers that, in all his knowledge, he does not finally know."[17] At this point Kircher and Dewey's views of philosophy tend to merge for, as we have seen, philosophy for Dewey meant a love of wisdom.

For reasons explained in previous chapters, the discipline of educational philosophy developed-at least partially—as a derivative of the academic field of philosophy in general. While this is understandable, the result has often been that educational philosophers were particularly susceptible to the pitfalls of discipleship described earlier. Those adhering to the "implicative" or "applicative" views of educational philosophy often became unwitting victims of their appropriated system or approach. As illustrated in the narrative that introduced this chapter, even Dewey's vision is not immune. Kircher contends that both Bode and Kilpatrick allowed themselves to be victimized by their allegiance to their mentor. As described in the previous chapter, there has been a tendency among some of us associated with the Philosophy for Children program to be victimized by their reverence for Matthew Lipman and his very significant contributions to uniting philosophy and pedagogy. Still, Dewey's vision, and Lipman's program have much in common with Kircher's advocacy of the philosopher as pilgrim. Together they offer hope for the creation of an educational philosophy as an expansive discipline that successfully bridges the gulf between educational practice and theory.

THE QUESTION OF VISION

The suggestion that the philosopher ought to be more of a pilgrim than a disciple raises a number of interesting questions. Particularly, in light of earlier discussions suggesting that educational philosophers made a mistake in abandoning Dewey's vision, the question becomes how can one embrace Dewey's vision without succumbing to the pitfalls of discipleship and authoritarianism discussed previously? A related question concerns the possibility of developing a defensible moral vision without that vision evolving into a domineering and imposing dogma or meta-narrative. To put it another way, is it possible to avoid being gored by either the absolutists or relativistic horns of the dilemma? Is there any way for humankind to escape this either/or thinking? Dewey believes there is, suggesting that democracy as a way of life, that is, as a self-correcting community of inquiry, constitutes such a vision. Still, in an attempt to avoid being wounded by our own petard, each one of us must critically examine the vision that Dewey and others offer. For any vision to have merit, it must be our own rather than someone else's that we have appropriated. In an attempt to understand what Dewey and others mean by vision in this non-absolutistic sense and in our struggle to respond to the questions identified earlier, we turn now to a discussion of what other, more contemporary thinkers have to say about vision and prophecy.

First, the notion of "prophetic thought" as defined by Cornel West may be helpful. West, long recognized as an outstanding scholar known for his critique of American religious and philosophic thought, has more recently entered the public arena, seeking to reach an audience beyond his academic peers and students. In a recent work, published almost verbatim from his public lectures, West is attempting to achieve a "public" voice. In this little work, *Prophetic Thought in Postmodern Times*, West explains for a general audience what he means by "prophetic thought." "There are," he suggests, "four basic components, four fundamental features, four constitutive elements." The elements include Discernment, Connection, Tracking Hypocrisy, and Hope.

In regards to the first component—Discernment, West suggests that "prophetic thought must have the capacity to provide a deep and broad analytical grasp of the present in light of the past."[19] Much like the journeyer in Kafka's fable discussed in an earlier chapter, a deep understanding of the past is necessary for grasping the complexities of the present and for conceptualizing possible visions of the future that build upon and extend the best that the past and present have to offer. In short, a prophetic thinker must be a bit of a historian, developing a vision of what should be out of a sophisticated understanding of what has been and is.

The second component of "prophetic thought" concerns the necessity of human connection. Here West is suggesting that a prophetic thinker must relate to or connect with others. Rather than just considering humankind in the abstract, West suggests that prophetic thinkers must value and have empathy for fellow human beings. To West, "empathy is the capacity to get in contact with the anxieties and frustrations of others."[20] Such empathy is in short supply in our modern world. Like William James before him, West agonizes over the all too common tendency of individuals today to treat others as stereotypical objects rather than as fellow human beings worthy of respect. Philosophers, including educational philosophers, in their obsession with finding what Kircher called the philosopher's stone, have often ignored this element or component of prophetic thought. In their search for that one abstract and absolute truth or method for attaining the truth, philosophers, including educational philosophers, too often failed to connect with their fellow human beings. Infatuated with the so-called problems of philosophy, philosophers have lost touch with the problems of humankind.

This failure to connect can be seen in the complaint of many students in schools that their teachers just don't care. As Noddings explains, these students "feel alienated from their schoolwork, separated from the adults who try to teach them, and adrift in a world perceived as baffling and hostile."[21] Still, many teachers do care and work very hard to help students, but they are often "unable to make the connection that would complete caring relations with their students."[22] In many cases the teachers themselves have become victims of the desires of the educational theorists, including some educational philosophers, for establishing "teaching onto a firm scientific footing..." In this "drive to find one best way of getting people to learn," teachers and students lost the ability to connect with one another as persons. This "worship of method" is not new for "other thinkers have tried since the time of Descartes to substitute fool-proof method for the situated, living human being who think and decide."[23] In this search for the one best method, the humanity of both teachers and students has been denied, and they have become 'treatments' and 'subjects' in the most recent manifestation of *the* science of pedagogy.

While the relationship between the need for empathy with others and pedagogy is fairly obvious, equally important to the "prophetic thinker" is the ability to identify and make known "the gap between principles and practice, between promise and performance, between rhetoric and reality."[24] West identifies this third component of prophetic thought as a tracking of hypocrisy and suggests that it ought to be done in a self-critical rather than a self-righteous manner. Both courage and humility are necessary for us to boldly and defiantly point out human hypocrisy. As the death of Socrates so vividly illustrates, there are risks involved in challenging the assertions of those purporting to be wise; and as the life of Socrates exemplifies, even our most strongly felt beliefs must not be reified into dogma. We must retain our humility by pointing "out human hypocrisy while remaining open to having others point out that of [our] own."[25]

West explains that a prophetic thinker cannot be "one that [has] unmediated access to God."[26] Such a view does not deny for a prophetic thinker the necessity of faith, but suggests that prophetic thinkers place their faith in humankind's ability to learn from their mistakes and create better, more meaningful lives. To participate in this component of prophetic thought is to be open to opinions different than our own. By considering other points of view, new evidence may emerge that refutes part or all of the original stance. In scrutinizing this new evidence, it may prove to be inadequate or incorrect thus enhancing the original position. In either case, knowledge has been expanded, making progress possible.

One who claims unmediated access to God—or in more contemporary times to a dogmatic allegiance to *the* method of science—suffers from no such humility. Since such an individual knows the truth or at least the means of attaining the truth, it is unnecessary to consider other points of view. Such a dogmatic view contributes to ignorance since, as John Stuart Mill pointed out more than a century ago, those who refuse to consider other points of view do not truly understand their own. Without understanding other points of view, such individuals have no grounds for preferring their own point of view. Consider for the moment the possibility that the fundamentalist's belief is the absolute truth; or that the method of positivistic science will lead us to the truth. The question then becomes, is indoctrination the best way to ensure the acceptance of either of these perspectives by future generations? As Mill points out, even the absolute truth "unless it is suffered to be and actually is, vigorously and earnestly contested, it will by most of those who receive it, be held in the manner of prejudice, with little comprehension or feeling of its rational grounds."[27] If either the fundamentalist's or positivist's perspectives merits everyone's allegiance, that is, if it is the whole truth or the means for attaining the whole truth, then each new generation must internalize it and make it our own. For this to occur, these perspectives must compete in the free marketplace of ideas. Let the arguments for each perspective be given their fullest expression by one capable of presenting the best possible case for them. In turn, allow a fair and strong case for alternative points of view to be presented. Scrutinize all perspectives, including your own, to see how its rhetoric matches with reality. Admittedly, the freemarket of ideas where all voices have equal opportunity to be heard is an ideal yet to be fulfilled, but, as a crucial component of prophetic thought, it is worthy of humankind's best efforts. To achieve this ideal takes courage and humility, two characteristics of the third component of prophetic thinking West labels as tracking hypocrisy.

The fourth and perhaps most important component of prophetic thought is, simply, hope. West admits that, given the numerous and horrific examples of humankind's inhumanity to each other, it is hard to take hope seriously in the modern world. Still, we must talk about it for without hope, all thought, including the three previously discussed components of prophetic thought, is meaningless. As West explains

> To talk about human hope is to engage in an audacious attempt to galvanize and energize, to inspire and to invigorate world-weary people. Because that is what we are. We are world-weary; we are tired. For some of us there are misanthropic skeletons hanging in our closet. And by misanthropic I mean the notion that we have given up on the capacity to do anything right. The capacity of human communities to solve any problem.[28]

West suggests that "we must face that skeleton as a challenge, not a conclusion."[29] Even when confronted with numerous human atrocities and multiple failures at creating community, the prophetic thinker must keep foremost in mind "the notion that history is incomplete, that the world is unfinished, that the future is open-ended and that what we think and what we do can make a difference."[30] As West explains, if we abandon this faith, if we loose hope in this sense, all that is left is "sophisticated analysis." As noted earlier, some of the more extreme forms of postmodernism offer little more than a sophisticated analysis of our contemporary world.

As alluded to earlier, West's notion of prophetic thought is grounded in a very significant religious tradition associated with the Afro-American experience in the United States. Still, his advocacy of prophetic thought owes as much to John Dewey as it does to his own religious tradition. Given this, the question remains to what extent is prophecy or vision dependent upon metaphysical or religious absolutes? While David Purpel's thought is largely compatible with West's notion of prophetic thought, Purpel suggests that the lack of such a moral vision grounded in religious or metaphysical assumptions has produced, in his words "the moral and spiritual crisis in education." Purpel advocates that educators work within the prophetic tradition "to remind us of our highest aspirations, of our failures to meet them, and of the consequences of our responses to these situations."[31]

To this point, Purpel's view of prophecy is indistinguishable from that of West, but Purpel is not finished. Suggesting that educators as prophets "orient the educational process toward a vision of ultimate meaning," Purpel adds that educators who accept the role as prophet "must affirm then a set of sacred and moral principles—a mythos, a set of metaphysical or religious assumptions—or commit themselves to that which has ultimate meaning to them."[32] In the statement just quoted, Purpel comes perilously close to reifying the notion of prophetic thought or vision into a dogma. While he is careful to use "a set" rather than "the set" in referring to religious and moral principles and in suggesting that what has ultimate meaning may be up to the individual educator, the tone of the remarks suggests that there is some ultimate meaning that humankind is capable of creating or finding.

The problem here lies in the notion of "ultimate" meaning. If ultimate meaning refers to a set of beliefs that are individually, culturally, and contextually defined, then the issue of reification is not relevant. If "ultimate" meaning refers to some transcendent and universal entity then the question about reification seems appropriate. This question is raised here since Purpel's notion of prophetic thought or prophecy is rooted in a sophisticated understanding of the biblical prophets. Suggesting that these prophets had a voice because of their "capacity to foretell the future," Purpel explains that this capacity stemmed, in part, from their "keen understanding of how underlying forces [were] affecting events." In this way the biblical prophets served a similar function performed today by social scientists and the occasional public philosopher. In addition, Purpel suggests that since the prophets often "reflected and influenced community attitudes," their very act of publicly predicting the future contributed to its future manifestation. Perhaps most important these biblical prophets claimed "to have privileged communication with God, or at the very least to have special sensitivity to know God's will."[33] Clearly there is a need in the modern world for educators to emulate the biblical prophets in analyzing the past and present for the purpose of envisioning what the future could and should be. The question remains whether educators as prophets can effectively perform such a role if they cannot, as West suggests, "have unmediated access to God." As far as I can tell this is a question that Purpel does not address.

What Purpel does do is advocate that educators, or at least some of them, "speak in the prophetic voice that celebrates joy, love, justice, and abundance..." Purpel practices what he preaches laying out for us his vision of what society and education ought to be. Included among the six goals Purpel articulates as his educational credo—all of which are compatible with West's notion of prophetic thought—is "the cultivation and nourishment of the processes of meaning making." As Purpel explains, humankind is "intent on creating systems of thought that explain our past and guide our present and future."[34] Sounding very much like a pragmatist, Purpel further explains:

> The educational goal is not so much to teach a particular meaning systems but rather to teach for the process of responding to that challenge. Educators must remind themselves and their students that any civilization or any culture is a human construction; thus, it is intellectually unsound to encourage the notion that cultural institutions, values and beliefs are given....[35]

Purpel's educational credo is commendable, but he presents in such a way that suggests that this credo is non-negotiable. In presenting his credo, Purpel acknowledges the "twin dangers of being either dogmatic or uncommitted."[36] If Purpel occasionally fails to successfully negotiate this moral tightrope, he consciously errs on the side of commitment. Further illustration of this emphasis on commitment is apparent in his call for educators to "facilitate the dialogue" so as to remind us of our culture's sacred commitments, and "how they are to be interpreted in light of particular situations, and what constitutes appropriate responses to them."[37] Such facilitating borders on manipulation. But as Purpel argues the line between education and indoctrination cannot always be clearly drawn.

While Purpel does not provide us with a definitive answer to the question regarding achieving a defensible moral vision in our postmodern world—in a world without metanarratives, his advocacy of the educator as prophet helps us appreciate the complexity of the problem. While Purpel's view can be interpreted to be grounded in religious or metaphysical first principles, the late Kenneth Benne provides us with a view of prophecy that is more consistent with a pragmatic view of knowledge and the universe. Offering a perspective that is largely compatible with the ideas of West, Benne distinguishes prophecy from prediction and foretelling. From Benne's perspective the prophet is a visionary who may, depending upon the circumstances,

> speak for viable and valid traditional values now threatened by current historical trends and fashions in life and in education. He or she may call for a reinterpretation of traditional values to make them more applicable to changed and changing conditions of life and learning. Or the prophet may speak for new values, ones that are potential, yet inadequately actualized in the contemporary, balanced imbalance of established powers and policies. Prophets may seek to persuade their audiences to integrate valid and viable—but now segregated and competing—values, both traditional and novel. They may urge others to support the integration of outlooks in making decisions about what should be done, not in a fantasized future but in the actuality of today, in behalf of a better tomorrow. In short, prophecy seeks to focus, clarify, and strengthen, rather than to discount and diminish, human volition as a determinant in the process of history.[38]

Benne's perspective of prophecy is similar to West's advocacy of prophetic thought. In what, in all likelihood, he knew to be his last work, Benne's *The Task of Post-Contemporary Education: Essays in Behalf of a Human Future* focuses on the questions:

> Can prophetic reeducation stimulate contemporary persons and cultures toward the control of technology and toward the creative mediation of conflicts in the interest of species' survival? Can educational policies and programs be created and employed to make a post-contemporary life for humankind more probable than it now appears to be?[39]

While not minimizing the difficulty of the task, the tone of Benne's last work is remarkably optimistic. Although Benne suggests some tentative solutions to the basic problems confronting the post-contemporary world (Benne prefers post-contemporary to postmodern), he adds that

> "Answers" that are both wise and viable for humankind will emerge only out of far-flung communal dialogues and collaborative projects. The dialogues and collaborations required must be sustained international, interreligious, interracial, interclass, intergender, and intergenerational conversations and cooperations, if their outcomes are to be both wise and effective.[40]

The interesting characteristic about both Benne's and West's—and to a lesser degree Purpel's—advocacy of prophecy is that each viewed it as more of a process for addressing the difficult problems that confront humankind in today's world than a set of answers or solutions to contemporary problems. Collectively their emphasis on process lends credence to answering in the affirmative to the question regarding the efficacy of a moral vision not grounded in some foundational metanarrative.

While the issues that revolve around prophecy or vision are of contemporary interest, they are not new. In a sense the ideas that collectively make up what West identifies as prophetic thought are similar to what John E. Smith characterizes as "America's Philosophical Vision." Perhaps the overarching theme that permeates this vision is the uniquely American emphasis on "the promise of the future over the significance of the past..." Once again William James succinctly captured the American society's capacity for hope suggesting that "we have a great stake in the more to come."[41] For a variety of historical, political, and geographic reasons, the many cultures that comprise what is known today as the United States have generally been more concerned with what tomorrow will bring than over what happened yesterday. This hopeful, rather optimistic characteristic of "American thought" has manifested itself in a number of ways.

Smith identifies three ways in which American philosophical thought manifests this forward-looking tendency. There is, first of all, a willingness on the part of American thinkers to be "open and receptive to points of view other than their own and they have welcomed the many different winds of philosophical doctrine from whatever quarter they have blown."[42] If Smith is correct in suggesting that such receptivity is characteristic of the spirit of American philosophy, then philosophy in general and educational philosophy in particular have abandoned this spirit during much of the twentieth century.

The second hallmark of philosophy in America, according to Smith, is change. Smith suggests that Americans were among the first to recog-

nize the reality of change and to appreciate the implications that the theory of evolution had for our concepts of knowledge and knowing. If, as
the theory of evolution suggests, change, more than permanency, is the
defining characteristic of our existence, then knowledge cannot be
thought of as some absolute or finite entity to be attained and passed on
intact to each new generation. In a world characterized by change, there
are no absolute or permanent truths, only warranted assertions arrived at
through a process of self-corrective inquiry and agreed upon as the most
reasonable answer to date by those most qualified to judge. Though he
phrases it a bit differently, Smith suggests that American philosophers
since the time of Pierce have been struggling with a version of the themes
that characterize this work in general and this chapter in particular.
According to Smith, American philosophers were among the first to wres-
tle with the question: "how is it possible to take seriously the facts of
change and fallibility in the knowing situation and at the same time avoid
a relativism which suggests that in essence we have no knowledge at all?"[43]

The third unique focus of American philosophy is on ideas that are
relevant, that is, on ideas that, "James liked to say, 'count' in any attempt
to deal with some issue or problem."[44] American philosophy has, suggests
Smith, always had a practical bent. This can best be seen "in the conception of intelligence as problem-solving where the task is to discover not
how much we know but precisely what items in our store of knowledge
count or have relevance for dealing with the problems at hand."[45] Here,
too, if relevance is a characteristic of the American philosophic spirit, both
philosophy and educational philosophy have abandoned that spirit in
recent years.

Smith considers the American philosophical vision to be largely a
pragmatic one. While some may challenge his characterization of the
American philosophical spirit as being too narrow, others, most notably
Foucault, suggest that intellectual prophecy is no longer a viable option
in today's diverse and fragmented world. Foucault's pronouncement that
the universal intellectual "as the bearer of universal values" has been
replaced by the specific intellectual—the expert or savant in a specific
domain—is accurate enough, but in suggesting that intellectual prophecy is gone forever, Foucault is engaging in the delphic or prophetic
thought he condemns. To his credit, Foucault recognizes that even the
specific intellectual can and should use her local and professional knowledge to impact areas that transcend her professional, class, and geographic domains.[46]

In conjunction with the positions articulated by West, Benne, and
others, the point emphasized here is that it remains an open question

whether the specific knowledge of the pragmatic philosopher can or should evolve into a more expansive vision. In short, the extent that prophetic thought can transcend local, class, and professional boundaries cannot be determined a priori. It is the position taken in this chapter and work that such prophetic thought, grounded in West's four elements or similar components, merits the chance to succeed or fail. Rather than presume that universal prophecy is passé, why not encourage visionary thought that consciously seeks to transcend temporal and cultural boundaries. To paraphrase an argument presented by Nicholas Burbules, why not replace a rather extreme postmodern presumption that intellectual prophecy is no longer possible or the rather naive Enlightenment faith in its efficacy with "a pragmatic, contextual, fallibilistic perspective" that favors hope over despair and suggests that a more positive vision of the future is a necessary, though not sufficient, first step in creating a better, more humane world.[47] Why not embrace this Deweyian perspective long enough to see if it works?

Whether this pragmatic perspective embodies the whole of the American philosophic spirit is problematic, but this vision of philosophy is consistent with the prophetic thought advocated by West, Purpel, and Benne. As noted in the previous chapter, Philosophy for Children at its best exemplifies this spirit, and, as demonstrated in the next section, there are other exemplars of what this prophetic and pragmatic vision offers the all but moribund field of educational philosophy.

EXEMPLARY SCHOLARSHIP IN EDUCATIONAL PHILOSOPHY: TWO EXAMPLES

Much of this chapter, indeed much of this entire work, criticizes the past and present state of educational philosophy. Such a critical stance is necessary for a work that purports to examine the origins of this relatively young field of study, and to suggest where it is and where it ought to be. While it is clear that the field is not healthy, educational philosophers cannot afford to wallow in pessimism. Educational philosophers need to realize that their field is in jeopardy, but we must not lose hope for, to paraphrase Cornel West, the future is not preordained. In short, while the field will not survive as it is or as it has been, its fate is largely in the hands of those of us who consider ourselves to be educational philosophers. While it is not possible for anyone to offer a sure cure for what ails the field of educational philosophy, the purpose of this work is to encourage educational philosophers to embrace the prophetic vision that many of their mentors and others that preceded them rejected earlier in this century. In short, this work can be seen as an invitation for educational philosophers to return to Dewey's prophetic vision of philosophy as the starting point for reconstructing the field.

What is needed, to paraphrase William Van Til, is not more disciples of Dewey, but serious students of his thought who extend, reconstruct, and apply Dewey's insights in light of the educational and social problems facing humankind today. As illustrative examples of what educational philosophy can and should be, recent works by Nicholas Burbules and Gerald Grant are discussed below. While these works are vastly different, both follow in the Deweyian vision of what philosophy, particularly educational philosophy, should be. Just as these works emulate, rather than mimic, Dewey's vision, they are examples worthy of emulation for others concerned about the moribund nature of their chosen field.

DIALOGUE IN TEACHING

In an earlier chapter, Ernest Bayles's plea for educational philosophers to deal "directly and forthrightly with problems of education" was discussed. Too few heard and responded to Bayles's plea during the last thirty years, but a recent work by Nicholas C. Burbules exemplifies the kind of scholarship that Bayles suggests educational philosophers ought to be doing. As Jonas Soltis notes in his foreword to *Dialogue in Teaching: Theory and Practice*, Burbules draws upon the theories of Baktin, Freire, Gadamer, Habermas, Vygotsky, and Wittgenstein as well as Dewey to illuminate the relationships among dialogue, teaching, and democracy. Burbules offers a sophisticated analysis of teaching through dialogue, but, more importantly, he makes it accessible to nonphilosophers.

In examining the relationship between dialogue and teaching, Burbules suggests that associating dialogue with *the* so-called Socratic method is misleading. He argues that there is no such thing as *the* Socratic method since this so-called method means different things to different people. Consistent with Burbules argument is the discussion of the Socratic method Scott Turow offers in his book, *One L.* In describing his trials and tribulations as a first-year law student, Turow suggests that, at Harvard Law School, the Socratic method meant everything from the fierce, intimidating teaching style immortalized by Professor Kingsfield in *The Paper Chase* to the often frustrating discussions conducted by a professor who questioned everything—every decision, every argument, and every brief—seemingly never arriving at a sound conclusion. Sensitive to the criticism that dialogue itself has been reified as *the* ultimate pedagogical device or technique, Burbules argues that the Socratic method is "not truly a 'method' at all but a repertoire of dialogical approaches that the skilful teacher knows how to select and adapt to varied pedagogical circumstances."[48]

According to Burbules, "dialogue is an activity directed toward discovery and new understanding which stands to improve the knowledge, insights, or sensibilities of its participants."[49] This can occur "even when the roles...do not break out neatly as 'teacher and student.' Dialogue represents a continuous, developmental, communicative interchange through which we stand to gain fuller apprehension of the world, ourselves, and one another."[50] In certain instances, those conducting the dialogue may have an intended goal in mind, such as sharing an already formulated insight or seeking input in response to particular questions. While a certain amount of orchestration is inevitable and at times desirable, dialogues often take on a life of their own that no one can predict or control. When this occurs none of the participants, including the conductor, knows exactly where the dialogue is heading or whether it will be successful or not. There are risks involved in such a process, but there are also opportunities for breaking new ground, for gaining new insights, and for expanding our views of the world and of ourselves.

In dialogue, a participant "may prefer a certain position but does not hold to it non-negotiably."[51] As Burbules explains, "the spirit of dialogue is, in short, the ability to hold many points of view in suspension, along with a primary interest in the creation of common meaning."[52] For the dialogue to work—for the community of inquiry to be developed—there must be a level of reciprocity, as Burbules calls it, among all choosing to participate in the dialogue. This means that participants must commit to respecting both the person and the perspective of other participants as worthy of consideration. In short, "what we ask of others we must be prepared for them to ask of us; and what we expect of others we must expect of ourselves."[53] Without this kind of mutual respect a dialogue is not possible.

A related and equally necessary characteristic of dialogue is active, but voluntary participation. For dialogue to be pedagogical requires that all participants be actively involved. Active participation can take a variety of forms, but there must be opportunities for engagement, questioning, trying out new ideas, and learning diverse points of view. Participants in the dialogue must feel comfortable in posing questions, in challenging other points of view, and in volunteering a seemingly "off the wall" idea without fear of condemnation or ridicule. When these characteristics are present, "the dialogical relation has in itself a strongly pedagogical element, in which participants seek to teach and learn from one another; and the voluntary aspect of this participation is crucial, since a reluctant partner is not likely to gain, or contribute, anything at all."[54] As Burbules explains, "a successful dialogue involves a willing partnership and cooperation in the face of likely disagreements, confusions, failures, and misunderstandings."[55]

Burbules's analysis of what the dialogical relationship could and should be is similar to what we in the Philosophy for Children tradition refer to as a community of inquiry. Creating a classroom atmosphere conducive to the establishment of such a community of inquiry is a task worthy of educational philosophers. Understanding and appreciating dialogue as a powerful pedagogical tool is an important first step in reorienting educational philosophers toward this goal. In offering a scholarly yet readable analysis of dialogue and its relationship to teaching, Burbules exemplifies one kind of scholarship that educational philosophers ought to be doing. More significantly, when such a work is written by the editor of the best known and most prestigious journal in the field, there is reason to hope that the community of professional educational philosophers is finally ready to take seriously and deal forthrightly with the problems of education.

Burbules suggests that to deal with the problems of education is to deal with the problems of democracy. Such problems include enabling different individuals and groups

> to learn about and understand competing positions on issues and, while not always coming to agreement or consensus about them, grasp sufficiently the points of view of others so that the outcomes reached by democratic processes are acceptable, if not the most favorable to every group. In this sense, dialogue is essential to democracy.[56]

Burbules's suggestion that "the significance of philosophical questions about what is true, or good, or right, or beautiful needs to be assessed in terms of their relation to, and effect on, social life"[57] places him within the pragmatic, if not Deweyian tradition. Further indication that Burbules is a serious student of Dewey's thought can be seen in his unwillingness to fall prey either to the "antimodern presumption that dialogue must fail, or an Enlightenment faith that it must succeed..."[58] In advocating instead, "a pragmatic, contextual, fallibilistic perspective that regards the possibilities of dialogue with persistence and hope, while being prepared as well for its possible failure and breakdown,"[59] Burbules is practicing West's notion of prophetic thought.

Burbules explains that a defining question of his work was "whether a theory and practice of dialogue that respond to the postmodern critique are possible."[60] Burbules answers the question in the affirmative, suggesting

an approach to dialogue that challenges hierarchies and traditional conceptions of teacher and authority; that is tolerant and supportive of diversity; that does not rely on teleological presumptions of right answers and final truths; that does not rest on isolated individual efforts, but on mutual and reciprocal communicative relations; and that keeps the conversation open, both in the sense of open-endedness and in the sense of inviting a range of voices and styles of communication within it.[61]

Recognizing that navigating between a "fond utopianism" on the one hand and a "bitter cynicism" on the other is no easy task, Burbules argues that "it is possible to develop an account of pedagogical communication that responds sympathetically to the issues raised by postmodern critics, without abrogating the possibility and worth of the educational."[62] In addition to refraining from "prejudging the question, either positively or negatively, of whether and how pedagogical communication can succeed," such an account "must focus on the nature and value of the educational *process*, without reifying or constraining the range of possibilities that this process might actually yield in contexts of practice."[63]

Burbules suggests that properly constructed dialogue can meet these characteristics and more. Participants in such a dialogical relationship—or members of a community of inquiry— "must acknowledge the reality of conflicts and relations of domination that exist in our world and distort the conditions under which communication takes place."[64] Basically, Burbules is suggesting that the free marketplace of ideas often does not exist in the real world, but can serve as a guiding vision of that which participants in dialogical relationships should work toward. In this regard, Burbules notes that members of a community of inquiry "must be especially sensitive to the diversity of experience and modes of expression that participants bring to a communicative situation."[65]

Burbules offers a critical perspective—informed by an understanding of and appreciation for the postmodernist critique—often missing in others who champion dialogue as a powerful pedagogical tool. While noting that constructing meaningful dialogical relationships is fraught with difficulties, Burbules remains optimistic adding:

While it is often difficult to communicate and understand one another across differences, this very situation stands to teach us the most, since it can bring to our understanding the perspective, values, and experiences of a contrasting point of view. The fundamental tension underlying the dialogical relation is this: We need to be similar enough for communication to happen, but different enough to make it worthwhile.[66]

Burbules effectively debunks any illusions that dialogue is the miraculous panacea for the divisiveness that characterizes the postmodern world, but he argues that, when properly constructed, dialogical relationships can contribute to making a difference in our lives. In this sense, his work exemplifies prophetic thought at its best and provides us with an example of a scholarly work that deals forthrightly and honestly with a crucial educational issue.

HAMILTON HIGH

In an earlier chapter, reference was made to John Dewey's advice to a young acquaintance suggesting that he study sociology rather than philosophy if he wanted to understand and use philosophy. While such a comment appears puzzling at first blush, Gerald Grant's *The World We Created at Hamilton High* provides us with a contemporary and very poignant illustration of what Dewey might have intended. Grant, a professor of Cultural Foundations of Education and Sociology at Syracuse University, offers us more than just a biography of the deconstruction and transformations that Hamilton High, originally an elite public high school, experienced in the 1960s, '70s, and '80s. By conveying "how students and teachers felt as these social revolutions swept through their school,"[67] Grant brings to life the philosophical and policy issues that our society and schools are grappling with during the second half of this century. In addition, he brings into focus the school's role in shaping character and illustrates for us how academic scholarship can contribute to the creation of a positive—intellectual and moral—ethos in our schools.

In addition to providing "a sociologically informed history of Hamilton High,"[68] Grant illuminates for us "the dynamics involved in creating a particular climate or ethos."[69] In this way he not only offers us a powerful portrait of how multiple and sometimes conflicting beliefs and values interact to create a particular ethos or culture, but he also provides for us a model of how academics, especially those in professional education, can and should make a positive contribution to the creation of a strong positive ethos in our schools and universities.

What began in the late 1970s as a National Institute of Education project focusing on the question of "What makes a good school?" eventually crystallized into both a historical portrait of a high school and an advocacy of a process for reconstructing schools into moral and intellectual communities. Grant explains that the defining moment leading to the development of the current work occurred in 1982 while characterizing Hamilton High to a group of school superintendents "as a place that had become more democratic, but also more bureaucratic, more adversarial, and officially value neutral."[70] Following Grant's suggestion that such an environment was less than ideal for adolescents, one of the superintendents asked him what he would do if he became principal of such a school. To this provocative question Grant responded:

> I would try to hire the best anthropologist I could find who could pass for a teenager. I would turn him or her loose in the school for several months with the aim of writing a portrait of the moral life of the community. Then I would use that report to initiate a dialogue with all the members of the polity—student, parents, teachers, and staff. I would ask them, Is this portrait true? Is this the best we can do? If we repeated this experiment five or ten years from now, what kind of school would you hope to see reflected in it?[71]

Grant never became principal of Hamilton High, but he did teach an urban anthropology course there beginning in the spring of 1984. Since hiring a pubescent anthropologist was not feasible, Grant decided to teach the high school students to be amateur anthropologists. Students could be taught "to observe, to take notes, to interview, to analyze data..." and "their findings could be used to raise critical questions about how to improve the quality of life in the school."[72] Grant indicates that these students did some stunning projects, and—along with his and other assistants' observation of this school for several years, his own experience as a teacher there in 1984 and 1985, plus "subsequent work with teachers and staff (of Hamilton High) in examining the implications of that research"[73]—enabled him to develop this biography of Hamilton High and to contribute to the ongoing task of creating a strong, positive ethos there.

In selecting this school as the subject for this biography, Grant chose well for Hamilton High "is America in microcosm. Hamilton High experienced all the overlapping social revolutions that fell, in a particularly powerful way, on schools in this society in the last thirty years."[74] In helping us to understand and reflect upon this difficult period of American history and education, *The World We Created at Hamilton High* is an unqualified success. Though Grant accurately portrays the intellectual chaos and moral relativism that characterized Hamilton High during these turbulent decades, he does not wallow in despair. Out of the deconstruction of the original white, suburban, upper-middle class ethos of Hamilton High came the opportunity to create a new positive ethos that more appropriately reflects the polity that now constitutes the school. In describing Hamilton High of the 1970s and 1980s as bowing down to the twin deities of bureaucratic legalism and therapeutic contractualism, Grant suggests that this school and others like it operated without a vision of what they could or should be. According to Grant, "bureaucratic legalism was the primary expression of the moral order of the school... If something was not legally forbidden it was usually assumed to be tolerated, or at least it was possible to make a stiff argument that it was."[75] The student handbook, rather than explaining to students Hamilton High's intellectual and moral mission, announced to them in legalistic terms the criminal behavior that was not allowed. As Hamilton High and other schools turned to bureaucratic legalism to both fill the vacuum created by the deconstruction of the old order and as the solution to intellectual, moral, and sometimes physical chaos produced by the social and demographic upheavals of the time, visions of what education could and should be were the major casualties.

Accompanying this overreliance on bureaucratic legalism was the tendency to embrace an extreme relativism or "anything goes" attitude. At Hamilton High and at other schools this manifested itself in numerous ways. For example, the roles between teacher and therapist became blurred. Teachers, except on occasions where unequivocal legalistic mandates had been broached, often behaved—sometimes out of fear—like therapists. For example, rather than challenge a student caught cheating on moral grounds, teachers often looked the other way or referred the student to a counselor to find out why they chose to cheat. Having no moral or educational vision to guide them, both teachers and students often rebelled against oughts and shoulds "as an intrusion of external and coercive authoritarianism."[76] As Grant explains

> Therapeutic contractualism tends to relieve faculty of the responsibility of encouraging all students to live by worthy standards and to encourage the view that if a student gets in trouble it is a psychological problem to be dealt with in a therapeutic relationship rather than a failure of the community to morally educate.[77]

Grant found this reliance on bureaucratic legalism and therapeutic contractualism as manifestations of a corrosive individualism that dominated the school. While this ethos was pervasive, Grant refuses to abandon hope. In the tradition of West and other prophetic thinkers, he attempts "to provide a new cultural definition of our situation, to explain how our program for survival went askew, and to show how we may be able to go on."[78] Refusing to either be paralyzed by cynicism or to accept "the brittle moral formulas" favored by fundamentalists, Grant chose instead to believe in the possibility of Hamilton High reconstructing itself so as to create a community based on a strong positive ethos. Grant acted upon this belief by using his scholarly research to facilitate the development of such a positive ethos.

Grant's response to a superintendent's provocative question established the parameters for what became *The World We Created at Hamilton High*. As part of the arrangement for his teaching an urban anthropology course at Hamilton High, Grant agreed to share his research with the faculty and staff of the school. In doing so, he hoped "to produce a more truthful book," and "to initiate a process of reflection among teachers and staff about ways to improve their school."[79] Outlining what he had in mind at a meeting of the faculty in March of 1986, seventy-seven of those present, including the principal, supported his idea. They elected a committee of twelve to participate in this process, and this group began meeting regularly with Grant to discuss the history of their school. Realizing that "the school was too bureaucratized" the principal joined in, choosing to participate as a member but refusing to chair the group.

Meeting during the 1986–87 school year to discuss the research and to consider ways of improving the school, this committee initiated a bottoms-up approach to school reform. Once the space for serious dialogue on what Hamilton High could and should be had been established, Grant suggests that "the dialogue unfolded in five stages."[80] While the stages cannot be delineated with absolute precision,

> the process developed roughly in these phases: (1) testing of the need for change, (2) doubt and resistance, (3) emergence of belief that common action was possible, (4) development of shared meaning about desirable policies and practices, and (5) proposal of a strategy for school-wide change.[81]

Given the school's history and its extant bureaucratic culture, it is not surprising that a cynical, if not pessimistic attitude permeated the group's meetings during their first months of deliberation. As Grant explains, "the emergence of belief that change was possible and that common action could be effective did not arise in a dramatic or sudden way."[82] But attitudes did change as pessimism gave way to hope that things could be better. Hope emerged out of this dialogue and with it came the realization that for any meaningful change to take place the faculty as a whole had to be involved. With this insight came the establishment of plans for a school-wide forum to discuss issues surfacing during the committees' deliberations and to discuss a strategy for school-wide change proposed by the committee. Through this process the faculty developed shared meanings of what they thought Hamilton High could and should be. While its ethos is continually evolving, the faculty of Hamilton High agreed

> that they wanted the school to emphasize dignity and respect for all persons, to place a premium on academic excellence and seek to motivate all students, to underscore the intrinsic value of learning, to develop a strong community spirit and encourage everyone to do his or her best, and to value the basic virtues of honesty and integrity. Finally they saw need for a school that was a learning community for faculty as well as students, one that provided for the growth of faculty both intellectually and socially.[83]

Grant's role in creating this new world at Hamilton High should not be overlooked or overplayed. He was instrumental in initiating the process and in providing the historical portrait that grounded the reflections and discussions. Initially he convened the meetings of the committee of twelve, but was replaced by a math faculty member elected to chair the group. Grant's knowledge and wisdom came into play as his timely suggestions often moved the group toward a meaningful solution, but these solutions or resolutions emerged through deliberations of the group. Perhaps his most important contribution was his faith in the power of dialogue to rejuvenate those for whom Hamilton High constituted a major part of their lives. By creating a space for dialogue, Grant rekindled the hope that it was still possible to remake Hamilton High into the kind of school that the faculty, students, and parents wanted. Rather than informing the faculty and staff of Hamilton High of what they should do, Grant initiated a process that enabled and invigorated the polity of Hamilton High to envision and create their own positive ethos.

In facilitating the emergence of a hopeful vision of what Hamilton High could and should be, Grant exemplifies the prophetic thought of West and others. In helping others to develop a positive vision of the future, Grant exemplifies public philosophy in the Deweyian tradition. In contributing to the creation of a better world at Hamilton High and in analyzing the factors that contributed to such a creation, Grant provides us with a model of educational philosophy worthy of emulation. In his work, as in that of Burbules, the process or dialogue is emphasized. In this sense these two exemplary cases of educational philosophy illustrate what is meant by the philosopher as pilgrim. While both Grant and Burbules demonstrate a commitment to a vision of what should be, theirs is a faith in dialogue as a process or processes that enable humankind to create and recreate their worlds. Such a vision allows, even compels one to act, but the process is a self-corrective one that must never be reified. In short, the process, much like the pilgrim's unconsummated quest, is never-ending.

CONCLUDING REMARKS

As stated in the introductory chapter of this work, an attempt has been to made to offer an interpretive history of the field of educational philosophy—what its been, where it is, and what it ought to be. Implicit in this historical analysis is the belief that educational philosophy as it is and has been will not survive much longer. Some suggest that it is too late to prevent the demise of the field, but, in remaining true to West's fourth element of prophetic thought, I refuse to abandon hope. In a sense, this work has been written to share a very personal belief that the study of educational philosophy can still play a significant role in creating the kind of educational institutions and through them the kind of society that honors and cherishes the best of humankind. This final chapter suggests—in sketching the role of the educational philosopher as pilgrim and in providing exemplary examples of contemporary educational philosophers whose work approximates this ideal—that it is not too late to reconstruct the field.

Such reconstruction is not without risks, but the time has come for educational philosophers to deal honestly and forthrightly with the problems of education. The time has come for educational philosophers to focus on the classroom, both as instructors in institutions of higher education and as members of teams concerned with developing the pedagogical knowledge and skills of those choosing to enter the profession of teaching. As suggested in chapter 4, it is perhaps the ultimate irony that for educational philosophy to succeed in what logically should be its mission, that is, contributing to enhancement of the profession of teaching, it must abandon its own quest for academic status as a professional discipline. For educational philosophers to become significant players in the reconstruction of our educational system as well as our society, they must overcome their dependency on the parent discipline. Rather than mimicking professional philosophers housed in university academic departments, educational philosophers must embrace a mission that they are uniquely qualified to perform. Rather than denying the philosophical spirit by serving as a disciple of a particular person, system, or approach, educational philosophers need to focus on integrating pedagogical theory into practice. Rather than aspiring acceptance into the guild of academic philosophers, educational philosophers must cherish their role of enhancing the professing of teaching.

In an attempt to emulate Cornel West's notion of prophetic thought, I choose to conclude this work on an optimistic note. It is my hope that by developing the skills, dispositions, and knowledge necessary for the kind of dialogical instruction advocated by Burbules, Grant and Lipman, educational philosophers can still make a difference. In helping future educators to experience and appreciate the power of a self-corrective community of inquiry, it is my hope that educational philosophers can and will play a significant role in the continuing development and spread of democracy as a way of life. The extent to which educational philosophers fulfill this hope will, I believe, determine the fate of the field of educational philosophy.

Notes

CHAPTER 1 INTRODUCTION AND OVERVIEW

1. James S. Kaminsky, "The First 600 Months of Philosophy—1935–1985: A Deconstructionist History," *Educational Philosophy and Theory* 18:2(October 1986): 41.

2. Harold Rugg, *The Teacher of Teachers: Frontiers of Theory and Practice* (Westport, CT: Greenwood Press, Publishers, 1952), p. 4.

3. Ibid., p. 3.

4. Ibid., p. 10.

5. Ibid., p. 7.

6. Ibid., p. 21.

7. J. J. Chambliss, *The Origins of American Philosophy of Education: Its Development as a Distinct Discipline, 1808–1913* (The Hague, Netherlands: Martinus Nijhoff, 1968), p. 106.

8. George P. Schmidt, *The Old Time College President* (New York: Columbia University Press, 1930), p. 112.

9. James S. Kaminsky, "A Pre-History of Educational Philosophy in the United States: 1861 to 1914," *Harvard Educational Review* 62:2(Summer 1992: 181.

10. Harold Rugg, *The Teacher of Teachers*, p. 60.

11. William Barrett, "The Twentieth Century and Its Philosophy," in William Barrett and Henry D. Aiken, eds., *Philosophy in the Twentieth Century* (New York: Random House, 1962), pp. 29–31.

12. John S. Brubacher, "Introduction: Purpose and Scope of the Yearbook," in Nelson B. Henry, ed., *The Forty-First Yearbook of the National Society for the Study of Education: Philosophies of Education* (Chicago: The University of Chicago Press, 1942), p. 4.

13. James M. Giarelli and J. J. Chambliss, "The Foundations of Professionalism: Fifty Years of the Philosophy of Education in Retrospect," *Educational Theory* 41:3(Summer 1991): 269.

14. Harry S. Broudy, "Between the Yearbooks," in *The Eightieth Yearbook of the National Society for the Study of Education, Philosophy and Education* (Chicago: The National Society for the Study of Education, 1981), p. 25.

15. Kieran Egan, *Teaching as Story Telling: An Alternative Approach to Teaching and Curriculum in the Elementary School* (Chicago: The University of Chicago Press, 1986), p. 15.

16. Bruce Wilshire, *The Moral Collapse of the University: Professionalism, Purity, and Alienation* (Albany, NY: State University of New York Press, 1990), p. 64.

17. Burton J. Bledstein, *The Culture of Professionalism: The Middle Class and the Development of Higher Education in America* (New York: W. W. Norton and Company, Inc., 1976), p. 326.

18. Kaminsky, "The First 600 Months of Philosophy of Education," p. 41.

19. Steve Tozer, "PES and School Reform," *Educational Theory* 41:3(Summer 1991), p. 304.

20. Ernest L. Boyer, *Scholarship Reconsidered: Priorities of the Professoriate* (Princeton, NJ: The Carnegie Foundation for the Advancement of Teaching, 1990).

21. Cleo H. Cherryholmes, *Power and Criticism: Poststructural Investigations in Education* (New York: Teachers College Press, Columbia University, 1988), p. 11.

22. Richard Rorty, *Philosophy and the Mirror of Nature* (Princeton: Princeton University Press, 1979), p. 315.

23. Ibid. , p. 6.

24. Richard Rorty, *Objectivity, Relativism, and Truth: Philosophical Papers (volume 1)* (Cambridge: Cambridge University Press, 1992), p. 180.

25. Dalton B. Curtis, Jr., "Philosophy of Education and the Public Mind,"

presidential address at the Southwest Philosophy of Education Meeting, South Padre Island, Texas, November 1988, p. 1.

26. John Novak, "Review of John Westbrook's *John Dewey and American Democracy.*"

27. Richard J. Bernstein, "Dewey, Democracy: The Task Ahead of Us," in John Rachman and Cornel West, eds., *Post Analytic Philosophy* (New York: Columbia University Press, 1985), p. 50.

28. John Dewey, *Democracy and Education* (New York: Free Press, 1966), p. 324.

29. Ibid., p. 354.

30. OgJames Gouinlock, "Introduction to John Dewey's *The Public and Its Problems,* in JoAnn Boydston, ed, *John Dewey: The Later Works, 1925–1953,* vol. 2 (Carbondale and Edwardsville, IL: Southern Illinois Press, 1984), p. xxxviii.

31. See author's "Philosophy As Education: Reviving Dewey's Vision," *Educational Foundations,* 4:(Fall 1990): 5–16 for a fuller explanation of these issues.

32. Matthew Lipman, *Thinking in Education* (Cambridge: Cambridge University Press, 1991), p. 263.

33. Everett J. Kircher, "Philosophy of Education—Directive Doctrine or Liberal Discipline?" *Educational Theory* (1955), p. 222.

34. Ibid. , p. 229.

35. Ibid.

36. Kenneth D. Benne, *The Task of Post-Contemporary Education: Essays in Behalf of a Human Future* (New York: Teachers College Press, 1990); David Purpel, *The Moral and Spiritual Crisis in Education* (Granby, MA: Bergin and Garvey, Inc., 1989); Cornel West, *Prophetic Thought in Postmodern Times* (Monroe, ME: Common Courage Press, 1993).

37. John E. Smith, *America's Philosophical Vision* (Chicago: The University of Chicago Press, 1992), p. 3.

38. Nicolas C. Burbules, *Dialogue in Teaching: Theory and Practice* (New York: Teachers College Press, 1993); and Gerald Grant, *The World We Created at Hamilton High* (Cambridge, MA: Harvard University Press, 1988).

39. Steve Tozer, "Toward a New Consensus among Social Foundations Educators: Draft Position Paper of the American Educational Association Committee on Academic Standards and Accreditation," *Educational Foundations* 7:4(Fall 1993): 13.

CHAPTER 2 NINETEENTH CENTURY ORIGINS
OF EDUCATIONAL PHILOSOPHY

1. J. J. Chambliss, *The Origins of American Philosophy of Education: Its Development as a Distinct Discipline, 1808–1913* (The Hague, Netherlands: Martinus Nijhoff, 1968), p. 108.

2. Ibid., p. 106.

3. Ibid., p. 8.

4. Ibid., p. 10.

5. Ibid.

6. Ibid., pp. 36–37.

7. James M. Giarelli and J. J. Chambliss, "The Foundations of Professionalism: Fifty Years of The Philosophy of Education Society in Retrospect," *Educational Theory* 41:3 (Summer 91): 266.

8. Arthur E. Murphy, "The Situation in American Philosophy," in Brand Blanshard, *Philosophy in American Education: Its Tasks and Opportunities* (New York: Harper and Brothers Publishers, 1945), p. 44.

9. Ibid., p. 45.

10. Frederick Rudolph, *The American College and University: A History* (New York: Alfred A. Knopf, 1962), p. 221.

11. Norman S. Fiering, "President Samuel Johnson and the Circle of Knowledge," *William and Mary Quarterly*, 3rd series, 1971, 28(April), 233, as quoted in Frederick Rudolph, *Curriculum: A History of the American Undergraduate Course of Study Since 1636* (San Francisco: Josey Bass Publishers, 1977), p. 42.

12. Chambliss, *Origins of American Philosophy of Education*, p. 80.

13. John Dewey, *Democracy and Education* (New York: Free Press, 1966), p. 328.

14. See James M. Giarelli, "Philosophy, Education, and Public Practice," in *Philosophy of Education* 1990, David Ericson, ed., (Normal, IL: The Philosophy of Education Society, 1991), p. 35; Brian Patrick Hendley, *Dewey, Russell, Whitehead: Philosophers as Educators* (Carbondale, IL: Southern Illinois University Press, 1986); and the author's "Philosophy *AS* Education: Reviving Dewey's Vision," *Educational Foundations* (Fall 1990): 5–16.

15. Cornel West, *The American Evasion of Philosophy: A Genealogy of Philosophy* (Madison: University of Wisconsin Press, 1989), p. 37.

16. Ibid., p. 36.

17. Ibid., p. 73.

18. Ibid., p. 76.

19. Ibid., p. 73.

20. Gladys Bryson, "The Emergence of the Social Sciences from Moral Philosophy," *International Journal of Ethics* 42(April 1932): 304–323.

21. Daniel Walker Howe and Wilson Smith provide scholarly discussions of the antebellum moral philosophies but only indirectly deal with the course itself. Daniel Walker Howe, *The Unitarian Conscience:: Harvard Moral Philosophy, 1805–1861* (Cambridge: Harvard University Press, 1970) and Wilson Smith, *Professors and Public Ethics: Studies of Northern Moral Philosophers before the Civil War* (Ithaca: Cornell University Press, 1956).

22. "Original Papers in Relation to a Course of Liberal Education," *The American Journal of Science and Arts* 15(January 1829): 329.

23. Douglas Sloan, "Harmony, Chaos, and Consensus," *Teachers College Record* 73(December 1971): 240.

24. George P. Schmidt, *The Old Time College President* (New York: Columbia University Press, 1930), p. 140.

25. Ibid., p. 112.

26. Daniel Walker Howe, *The Unitarian Conscience*, p. 54.

27. George E. Peterson, *The New England College in the Age of the University* (Amherst: Amherst College Press, 1964), p. 16.

28. Daniel J. Wilson, *Science, Community, and the Transformation of American Philosophy, 1860–1930* (Chicago: The University of Chicago Press, 1990), p. 5.

29. Laurence R. Veysey, *The Emergence of the American University* (Chicago: The University of Chicago Press, 1965), p. 302.

30. Ibid., pp. 320–323.

31. Ibid., p. 198.

32. Ibid., p. 227.

33. Ibid., p. 231.

34. Ibid., p. 233.

35. Douglas Sloan, "The Teaching of Ethics in the American Undergraduate Curriculum, 1876–1976," in Sissela Bok and Daniel Callahan, eds., *Ethics Teaching in Higher Education* (New York: Plenum Press, 1980), p. 1.

36. Ibid., p. 9.

37. Morris Bishop, *Early Cornell*, 1865–1900 (Ithaca: Cornell University Press, 1962), p. 162.

38. Ibid., pp. 275–276.

39. Ibid.

40. Ibid., p. 277.

41. Sloan, "The Teaching of Ethics," pp. 6–7.

42. Ibid., p. 13.

43. Ibid., p. 15.

44. Ibid., p. 17.

45. Ibid.

46. Ibid.

47. James S. Kaminsky, "A Pre-History of Educational Philosophy in the United States: 1861 to 1914," *Harvard Educational Review* 62:2(Summer 1992): 181.

48. Ibid.

49. Ibid., p. 182.

50. Ibid., p. 180.

51. Ibid., p. 183.

52. Harold Rugg, *The Teacher of Teachers: Frontiers of Theory and Practice in Teacher Education* (Westport, CT: Greenwood Press, Publishers, 1952), p. 24.

53. Ibid., p. 44.

54. Ibid., p. 60.

55. Ibid., p. 28.

CHAPTER 3 EDUCATIONAL PHILOSOPHY IN THE TWENTIETH CENTURY

1. Henry D. Aiken, "The Fate of Philosophy in the Twentieth Century," in William Barrett and Henry D. Aiken, eds., *Philosophy in the Twentieth Century* (New York: Random House, 1962), p. 11.

2. William Barrett, "The Twentieth Century and Its Philosophy" in Barrett and Aiken, eds., *Philosophy in the Twentieth Century*, pp. 29–31.

3. Ibid., p. 34.

4. Ibid.

5. Arthur E. Murphy, "The Situation in American Philosophy," in Brand Blandshard, *Philosophy in American Education: Its Tasks and Opportunities* (New York: Harper and Brothers Publishers, 1945), p. 53.

6. Geraldine Joncich Clifford and James W. Guthrie, *Ed School: A Brief for Professional Education* (Chicago: University of Chicago Press, 1988), p. 143

7. John S. Brubacher, "Introduction: Purpose and Scope of the Yearbook," in Nelson B. Henry, ed., *The Forty-First Yearbook of the National Society for the Study of Education: Philosophies of Education* (Chicago: The University of Chicago Press, 1942), p. 4.

8. Harry S. Broudy, "How Philosophical Can Philosophy of Education Be?" *The Journal of Philosophy* 52(October 27, 1955): 618.

9. James M. Giarelli and J. J. Chambliss, "The Foundations of Professionalism: Fifty Years of the Philosophy of Education Society in Retrospect," *Educational Theory* 41:3(Summer 1991): 269.

10. Ibid.

11. John S. Brubacher, "Comparative Philosophy of Education" in Nelson B. Henry, ed., *The Forty-First Yearbook of the National Society for the Study of Education: Philosophies of Education* (Chicago: The University of Chicago Press, 1942), p. 292.

12. Mortimer J. Adler, "In Defense of the Philosophy of Education" in *41st NSSE Yearbook: Philosophies of Education*, p. 199.

13. Brubacher, "Comparative Philosophy of Education," p. 319.

14. Broudy, "How Philosophical Can Philosophy Be?", pp.614 and 621.

15. Ibid, p. 622.

16. Harry S. Broudy, "Between the Yearbooks" in *The Eightieth Yearbook of the National Society for the Study of Education, Philosophy and Education* (Chicago: The National Society for the Study of Education, 1981), p. 25.

17. Richard Pratte, "Analytic Philosophy of Education: A Historical Perspective," in Jonas Soltis, ed., *Philosophy of Education Since Mid-Century* (New York: Teachers College Press, 1981), p. 22.

18. R. F. Dearden, "Philosophy of Education, 1952–82," British *Journal of Educational Studies* 30(February 1982): 61.

19. Ibid.

20. R.S. Peters, "Philosophy of Education" in Paul H. Hirst, ed., *Educational Theory and Its Foundational Disciplines* (London: Routledge and Kegan Paul, 1983), pp. 33 and 44.

21. Ibid., p. 44.

22. The 1972 NSSE yearbook, focusing on educational research, was titled *Philosophical Redirection of Educational Research.*

23. Jonas F. Soltis, "Introduction," in Jonas F. Soltis, ed., *The Eightieth Yearbook of the National Society for the Study of Education: Philosophy and Education* (Chicago: The University of Chicago Press, 1981), p. 7.

24. James M. Giarelli, "Philosophy, Education, and Public Practice," in *Philosophy of Education, 1990,* David Ericson, ed., (Normal, IL: The Philosophy of Education Society, 1991), p. 65.

25. G. Max Wingo *Philosophies of Education: An Introduction* (Lexington, MA: D.C. Heath and Company, 1974), p. i.

26. Ibid., p.3.

27. Ibid., p. 25.

28. Kieran Egan, *Teaching as Story Telling: An Alternative Approach to Teaching and Curriculum in the Elementary School* (Chicago: The University of Chicago Press, 1986), p. 6.

29. Ibid., pp. 8 and 10.

30. Ibid., p. 12.

31. Ibid., p. 15.

32. Ibid., p. 37.

33. Ibid., pp. 37 and 38.

34. Jonas F. Soltis, *An Introduction to the Analysis of Educational Concepts* (Reading, MA: Addison-Wesley Publishing Company, 1978), p. 5.

35. Ibid., p. 7.

36. Ibid.

37. Ibid., p. 20.

38. Ibid., p. 13.

39. Clive Beck, "North American, British and Australian Philosophy of Education from 1941 to 1991: Links, Trends, Prospects," *Educational Theory* 41:3(Summer 1991), p. 319.

40. Ibid.

CHAPTER 4 THE PROFESSIONALIZATION OF PHILOSOPHY AND EDUCATIONAL PHILOSOPHY

1. Russell Jacoby, *The Last Intellectuals: American Culture in the Age of Academe* (New York: The Noonday Press; Farrar, Straus, and Giroux, 1987), p. 147.

2. William Barrett, *Death of the Soul: From Descartes to the Computer* (Garden City, NY: Anchor Press, Doubleday, 1986), p. 3.

3. Ibid., p. 6.

4. Ibid., p. 7.

5. Ibid., p. 17.

6. Ibid., p. 18.

7. Bruce Wilshire, *The Moral Collapse of the University: Professionalism, Purity, and Alienation* (Albany, NY: State University of New York Press, 1990), pp. 38 and 39.

8. Ibid., p. xx.

9. Ibid., p. 64.

10. Burton J. Bledstein, *The Culture of Professionalism: The Middle Class and the Development of Higher Education in America* (New York: W. W. Norton and Company, Inc., 1976), p. 34.

11. Wilshire, *The Moral Collapse of the University*, p. 43.

12. Bledstein, *The Culture of Professionalism*, p. 31.

13. Ibid., pp. 4 and 5.

14. Ibid., p. 88.

15. Ibid., p. 3

16. Ibid., pp. 326 and 327.

17. Wilshire, *The Moral Collapse of the University*, p. 49.

18. Ibid., p. 99.

19. Ibid., p. 103.

20. Ibid., p. 105.

21. Janice Moulton, "A Paradigm of Philosophy: The Adversary Method" in Sandra Harding and Merrill B. Hintikka, eds., *Discovering Reality: Feminist Perspectives on Epistemology, Metaphysics, and Philosophy of Science* (Dordrecht, Holland: D. Reidel Publishing, 1983), pp. 156 and 157.

22. Ibid.

23. Ibid.

24. Wilshire, *The Moral Collapse of the University*, p. 117; quoted from the 1986 *Proceedings and Addresses of the American Philosophical Association.*

25. Ibid., p. 118.

26. Ibid., pp. 106 and 107.

27. Ibid., p. 112.

28. Ibid., p. 122.

29. James S. Kaminsky, "The First 600 Months of Philosophy of Education—1935–1985: A Deconstructionist History," *Educational Philosophy and Theory* 18:2(October 1986): 41.

30. Daniel Tanner, *Crusade for Democracy: Progressive Education at the Crossroads* (Albany, NY: State University of New York Press, 1991), p. xv.

31. Ibid., pp. 10 and 11.

32. Kaminsky, "The First 600 Months of Philosophy of Education," p. 41.

33. Nicholas C. Burbules, "Continuity and Diversity in Philosophy of Education: An Introduction," *Educational Theory* 41:3(Summer 1991): 257.

34. James M. Giarelli and J. J. Chambliss, "The Foundations of Professionalism: Fifty Years of The Philosophy of Education Society in Retrospect," *Educational Theory* 41: 3(Summer 1991): 268.

35. Ibid.

36. Ibid., p. 272.

37. Ibid., p. 273.

38. Steven Tozer, "PES and School Reform," *Educational Theory* 41:3 (Summer 1991): 304.

39. Ibid., p. 306.

40. Ibid., p. 307.

41. Ibid.

42. Thomas Nelson, "Philosophy of Education 1958–1980" in Margaret Buchmann and Robert Floden, eds., *Philosophy of Education 1991: Proceedings of the Forty-Seventh Annual Meeting of the Philosophy of Education Society* (Normal, IL: Philosophy of Education Society, 1992), p. 38.

43. Ernest L. Boyer, *Scholarship Reconsidered: Priorities of the Professoriate* (Princeton, NJ: The Carnegie Foundation for the Advancement of Teaching, 1990), p. 77.

44. Ibid., p. 1.

45. Ibid., p. 19.

46. Ibid., p. 21.

47. Ibid., p. 23.

48. Ibid., p. 22.

49. Ibid., p. 70.

50. Jonas F. Soltis, "Philosophy of Education for Educators: The Eightieth NSSE Yearbook," in Jonas F. Soltis, ed., *Philosophy of Education since Mid-Century* (New York: Teachers College Press, 1988), p. 118.

51. Geraldine Joncich Clifford and James W. Guthrie, *Ed School: A Brief for Professional Education* (Chicago: The University of Chicago Press, 1988), pp. 349 and 350.

52. Ibid., p. 365.

53. Richard Wisniewski, "Restructuring Schools of Education: The William Drake Lecture, 1990" in Wayne Willis, ed., *Proceedings of the Forty-First Annual Meeting of Southwestern Philosophy of Education Society* (Morehead, KY: Morehead State University, 1991), pp. 7 and 8.

54. Lee S. Shulman, "Reconnecting Foundations to the Substance of Teacher Education," in Jonas F. Soltis, ed., *Foundational Studies in Teacher Education* (New York: Teachers College Press, 1991), p. 11.

CHAPTER 5 POSTMODERNIST CRITIQUES OF EDUCATIONAL PHILOSOPHY

1. Landon E. Beyer and Daniel P. Liston, "Discourse or Moral Action? A Critique of Postmodernism," *Educational Theory* 42:4(Fall 1992): p. 374.

2. Paul Rabinow, ed., *The Foucault Reader* (New York: Pantheon Books, 1984), p. 249.

3. Cleo H. Cherryholmes, *Power and Criticism: Poststructural Investigations in Education* (New York: Teachers College Press, Columbia University, 1988), p. vii.

4. Ibid., p. 11.

5. Ibid., p. 13.

6. Richard J. Bernstein, *The New Constellation: The Ethical– Political Horizons of Modernity/Postmodernity* (Cambridge, MA: MIT Press, 1992), p. 51.

7. Ibid.

8. Ibid., p. 52.

9. Cherryholmes, *Power and Criticism*, p. 11.

10. Bernstein, *The New Constellation*, p. 8.

11. Ibid.

12. Ibid., p. 17.

13. Cornel West, *The American Evasion of Philosophy: A Genealogy of Philosophy* (Madison, WI: University of Wisconsin Press, 1989), pp. 199–200.

14. Bernstein, *The New Constellation*, p. 6.

15. West, *The American Evasion of Philosophy*, p. 200.

16. Bernstein, *Constellation*, p. 6.

17. West, *The American Evasion of Philosophy*, p. 197.

18. Richard Rorty, *Consequences of Pragmatism: (Essays: 1972–80)* (Minneapolis: University of Minnesota Press, 1983), p. 191.

19. Richard Rorty, *Philosophy and the Mirror of Nature* (Princeton: Princeton University Press, 1979), p. 3.

20. Ibid., p. 315.

21. Ibid., p. 317.

22. Richard Rorty, "Solidarity or Objectivity," in John Rajchman and Cornel West, eds., *Post-Analytic Philosophy* (New York: Columbia University Press, 1985) p. 3.

23. Ibid.

24. Richard Rorty, *Objectivity, Relativism, and Truth: Philosophical Papers (volume 1)* (Cambridge, England: Cambridge University Press, 1992), p. 21.

25. Ibid.

26. Ibid.

27. Ibid., p. 22.

28. Ibid.

29. Ibid., p. 67.

30. Ibid.

31. Rorty, *Philosophy and the Mirror of Nature*, p. 357.

32. Ibid., p. 6.

33. Ibid., p. 369.

34. Ibid., pp. 369–370

35. Ibid., p. 378

36. Rorty, "Solidarity or Objectivity," pp. 10 and 15.

37. Rorty, *Philosophy and the Mirror of Nature*, p. 369.

38. Ibid., p.378.

39. Ibid.

40. Charles Taylor, "Rorty in the Epistemological Tradition," p. 273 in Alan Malachowski, ed., *Reading Rorty: Critical Responses to Philosophy and the Mirror of Nature (and Beyond)* (Cambridge, MA: Basil Blackwell Ltd., 1990).

41. Ibid.

42. Rorty, *Objectivity, Relativism, and Truth*, p. 13.

43. Ibid., p. 181.

44. Ibid., p. 180.

45. Ibid.

46. Ibid.

47. Ibid., p. 13.

48. Ibid., p. 14.

49. Ibid.

50. Ibid.

51. Ibid., p. 212.

52. Ibid., p. 14.

53. Ibid., p. 34.

54. Benjamin Barber, *Strong Democracy: Participatory Politics for a New Age* (Berkeley: University of California Press, 1984), p. 4.

55. Ibid.

56. Ibid.

57. Ibid., pp. 24–25.

58. Rorty, *Objectivity, Relativism, and Truth*, p. 204.

59. Ibid., p. 206.

60. Ibid., p. 207.

61. Beyer and Liston, "Discourse or Moral Action? A Critique of Postmodernism," p. 371.

62. Ibid., p. 375.

63. Ibid.

64. Ibid., p. 379.

65. Ibid., p. 380.

66. Cherryholmes, *Power and Criticism*, p. 143.

CHAPTER 6 PHILOSOPHY *AS* EDUCATION: REVIVING DEWEY'S VISION

1. James M. Giarelli, "Philosophy and the mid-1980's," unpublished paper presented at Middle Atlantic States Philosophy of Education Society and the Ohio Valley Philosophy of Education Society, November 1, 1986, Pittsburgh, Pennsylvania, p. 1.

2. Robert B. Westbrook, *John Dewey and American Democracy* (Ithaca: Cornell University Press, 1991), p. 171

3. Ibid., p. 203.

4. Ibid., p. vi.

5. Ibid., p. 36.

6. This quotation as well as much of the information in this brief introduction were derived from John Novak's Review of John Westbrook's *John Dewey and American Democracy*.

7. John Dewey, *Experience and Education* (New York: Collier Macmillan Publisher, 1963).

8. John Dewey, *Democracy and Education* (New York: Free Press, 1966), p. 324.

9. Ibid., p. 354.

10. John Dewey, "Philosophy and Democracy," in Jo Ann Boydston, ed., *John Dewey: The Middle Works, 1899–1924*, vol. 11 (Carbondale and Edwardsville, IL: Southern Illinois University Press, 1984), p. 41.

11. Ibid., p. 43.

12. Ibid.

13. Ibid., p. 44.

14. Ibid., p. 45.

15. Ibid., p. 43.

16. John Dewey, "The Need for a Recovery of Philosophy," in Jo Ann Boydston, ed., *John Dewey: The Middle Works, 1899–1924,* vol. 10 (Carbondale and Edwardsville, IL: Southern University Press, 1984), p. 48.

17. Dewey, *Democracy and Education*, p. 354.

18. Ibid., p. 331.

19. Ibid., p. 328.

20. Ibid., p. 329.

21. Ibid., p. 328.

22. Richard J. Bernstein, "Dewey, Democracy: The Task Ahead of Us," in John Rajchman and Cornel West, eds., *Post-Analytic Philosophy* (New York: Columbia University Press, 1985), p. 50.

23. Dewey, *Democracy and Education*, p. 328.

24. John Dewey, *The Public and Its Problems* (New York: Henry Holt and Company, 1927), p. 86.

25. Ibid., p. 87.

26. Ibid., p. 91.

27. Henry S. Levinson, *Santayana, Pragmatism, and the Spiritual Life* (Chapel Hill: University of North Carolina Press, 1992), p. 254.

28. Dewey, *The Public and Its Problems*, p. 109.

29. OgJames Gouinlock, "Introduction to John Dewey's *The Public and Its Problems,*" in JoAnn Boydston, ed., *John Dewey: The Later Works, 1925–1953,* vol. 2 (Carbondale and Edwardsville, IL: Southern Illinois Press, 1984), p. xxxix.

30. John Dewey, *The Public and Its Problems*, in JoAnn Boydston, ed., *John Dewey: The Later Works, 1925–1953,* vol. 2 (Carbondale and Edwardsville, IL: Southern Illinois Press, 1984), p. 350.

31. Ibid., p. 330.

32. Richard J. Bernstein, *John Dewey* (New York: Washington Square Press, Inc., 1966), pp. 138–139

33. Ibid., p. 139.

34. John Dewey, "The Public and Its Problems," in Boydston, ed., *The Later Works*, p. 325.

35. Ibid., p.328.

36. Bernstein, *John Dewey*, pp. 134–135.

37. Gouinlock, "Introduction to John Dewey's *The Public and Its Problems*," p. xxxvi.

38. Bernstein, *Dewey*, p. 136.

39. Ibid., p. 135.

40. Gouinlock, "Introduction," p. xxxviii.

41. Dewey, "The Public and Its Problems," p. 350.

42. Ibid., p. 365.

43. Ibid.

44. Ibid., p. 368.

45. Benjamin Barber, *Strong Democracy: Participatory Politics for a New Age* (Berkeley: University of California Press, 1984), p. 265.

46. Ibid., p. 152.

47. Ibid., p. 211.

48. Ibid., p. 188.

49. Ibid., p. 261.

50. Ibid., p. 265.

51. Ibid., p. 175.

52. Ibid., p. 307.

53. Bernstein, *Dewey*, p.141.

54. Ibid., p. 143.

55. Ibid., pp. 143–144.

56. Ibid., p. 144.

57. Westbrook, *John Dewey*, p. 508.

58. Ibid., p. 540.

59. Ibid.

60. Dewey, *Experience and Education*, p. 6.

61. John Dewey, *Democracy and Education*, p. 328.

CHAPTER 7 PHILOSOPHY FOR CHILDREN: INPLEMENTING DEWEY'S VISION

1. Matthew Lipman, *Harry Stottlemeier's Discovery* (Montclair , N.J.: First Mountain Foundation, 1982), 1. All subsequent quotations in this section come from page 1 and 4.

2. This section of the essay including the lengthy excerpt from page 4 of *Harry Stottlemeier' Discovery* appeared in Tony W. Johnson, *Philosophy for Children: An Approach to Critical Thinking* (Bloomington, Indiana: Phi Delta Kappa Educational Foundation, 1984), pp. 7–8.

3. Ronald F. Reed and Ann F. Richter, "Matthew Lipman: Restoring the Connection Between Education and Philosophy," in James J. Van Patton, ed., *Academic Profiles in Higher Education* (New York: Edwin Mellen Press, 1992), p. 210.

4. An earlier draft of the information appearing in this section can be found in Tony W. Johnson, *Philosophy for Children: An Approach to Critical Thinking* (Bloomington, IN: Phi Delta Kappa Educational Foundation, 1984), pp. 18–27. In turn, this discussion of dialogue and the community of inquiry was derived from Matthew Lipman, Ann Margaret Sharp, and Frederick Oscanyan, *Philosophy in the Classroom* (Philadelphia: Temple University Press, 1980).

5. Reed and Richter, "Matthew Lipman: Restoring the Connection Between Education And Philosophy," pp. 204–206.

6. Matthew Lipman, "Dramatizing Philosophy," unpublished manuscript, 1993, p. 17.

7. Ibid., p. 37.

8. Ibid.

9. Ibid., p. 279.

10. Ibid., p. 59.

11. Ibid., p. 60.

12. Ibid., p. 65.

13. Ibid.

14. Ibid., p, 22.

15. Ibid., p. 23.

16. Ibid., p. 30.

17. Matthew Lipman, "On Writing a Philosophical Novel," in Ann Margaret Sharp and Ronald F. Reed, eds., *Studies in Philosophy for Children: Harry Stottlemeier's Discovery* (Philadelphia: Temple University Press, 1992), p. 4.

18. Ibid.

19. Ibid.

20. Matthew Lipman, *Philosophy Goes to School* (Philadelphia: Temple University Press, 1988) p. 12.

21. Ibid., p. 11.

22. Ibid., p. 17.

23. Lipman, "Dramatizing Philosophy," p. 240.

24. Matthew Lipman, *Thinking in Education* (Cambridge: Cambridge University Press, 1991), p. 163.

25. Lipman, "Dramatizing Philosophy," p. 293.

26. Lipman, *Thinking in Education*, p. 163.

27. Lipman, "Dramatizing Philosophy," p. 196.

28. Ibid., p. 197.

29. Ibid.

30. Ibid., p. 198.

31. Lipman, *Thinking*, p. 222.

32. Ibid.

33. Ibid.

34. Lipman, "Dramatizing Philosophy," pp. 170–171.

35. Ibid., p. 211.

36. Lipman, *Thinking*, p. 263.

37. Henry Giroux, *Teachers as Intellectuals: Toward a Critical Pedagogy of Learning* (Granby, MA: Bergin and Garvey Publishers, Inc., 1988), p. 16.

38. Jane Roland Martin, *Reclaiming a Conversation: The Ideal of the Educated Woman* (New Haven, CT: Yale University Press, 1985), p. 175.

39. Lipman, *Philosophy Goes to School*, p. 43.

CHAPTER 8   EDUCATIONAL PHILOSOPHY: DISCIPLESHIP OR PILGRIMAGE

1. William Van Til, "John Dewey Disciples," *Educational Leadership* 8:3 (December 1949) 202.

2. Ibid., p. 201.

3. Ibid.

4. Ibid., pp. 201–202.

5. Everett J. Kircher, "Philosophy of Education—Directive Doctrine or Liberal Discipline?" *Educational Theory* (1955), p. 220.

6. John E. Smith, *America's Philosophical Vision* (Chicago: The University of Chicago Press, 1992), p. 193.

7. Kircher, "Philosophy of Education—Directive Doctrine or Liberal Discipline?" p. 221.

8. Ibid.

9. Ibid., p. 222.

10. Ibid., p. 221.

11. Ibid., p. 224.

12. Ibid., p. 223.

13. Ibid.

14. Ibid.

15. Ibid., p. 226.

16. Ibid., p. 229.

17. Ibid.

18. Cornel West, *Prophetic Thought in Postmodern Times* (Monroe, Maine: Common Courage Press, 1993), p. 3.

19. Ibid.

20. Ibid., p. 5.

21. Nel Noddings, *The Challenge to Care in Schools* (New York: Teachers College Press, 1993), p. 2.

22. Ibid.

23. Ibid., p. 7.

24. West, *Prophetic Thought*, p. 5.

25. Ibid.

26. Ibid.

27. John Stuart Mill, "On Liberty" in *Great Books of the Western World* (Chicago: Encyclopaedia, Inc., 1952) vol. 43, p. 292.

28. West, *Prophetic Thought*, p. 6.

29. Ibid.

30. Ibid.

31. David Purpel, *The Moral and Spiritual Crisis in Education* (Granby, MA: Bergin and Garvey Publishers, Inc., 1989), p. 104.

32. Ibid., p. 105.

33. Ibid., p. 108.

34. Ibid., pp. 114–115.

35. Ibid.

36. Ibid., p. 113.

37. Ibid., p. 110.

38. Kenneth D. Benne, *The Task of Post-Contemporary Education: Essays in Behalf of a Human Future* (New York: Teachers College Press, 1990), p. x.

39. Ibid., p. xiii.

40. Ibid.

41. Smith, *America's Philosophical Vision*, p. 3.

42. Ibid., p. 196.

43. Ibid., p. 200.

44. Ibid., p. 193.

45. Ibid., p. 205.

46. Paul Rabinow, ed., *The Foucault Reader* (New York: Pantheon Books, 1984), pp. 67–74.

47. Nicholas C. Burbules, *Dialogue in Teaching: Theory and Practice* (New York: Teachers College Press, 1993), p. 160.

48. Ibid., pp. x–xi.

49. Ibid., p. 8.

50. Ibid.

51. Ibid., p. 19.

52. Ibid.

53. Ibid., p. 82.

54. Ibid., p. 27.

55. Ibid., p. 19.

56. Ibid., p. 14.

57. Ibid., p. 2.

58. Ibid., p. 160.

59. Ibid.

60. Ibid., p. 7.

61. Ibid.

62. Ibid., p. 31.

63. Ibid.

64. Ibid.

65. Ibid.

66. Ibid.

67. Gerald Grant, *The World We Created at Hamilton High* (Cambridge, MA: Harvard University Press, 1988), p. 6.

68. Ibid., p. 5.

69. Ibid., p. 3.

70. Ibid., p. 4.

71. Ibid.

72. Ibid.

73. Ibid., p. 5.

74. Ibid., pp. 5–6.

75. Ibid., p. 183.

76. Ibid., p. 184.

77. Ibid., p. 185.

78. Ibid., p. 1.

79. Ibid., p. 235.

80. Ibid., p. 248.

81. Ibid.

82. Ibid., p. 20.

83. Ibid., p. 253.

Subject Index

Index of Names